The Watch Buff's Book of Trivia

465 FUN FACTS ABOUT TIMEPIECES

NORMA BUCHANAN

Watch Buff Books
Wallingford, Connecticut

To Joe, the best husband of all time

CONTENTS

INTRODUCTION

To many people, a watch is a mere convenience, no more noteworthy than an eggbeater or a flush toilet. Others know differently. In the five centuries they've been around, watches have played more roles in our lives than any other object ever invented. They are, of course, timekeepers, helping us to get to work on time and to cook our spaghetti to *al dente* perfection. But they're also status symbols, tokens of love or appreciation, testaments to individual ingenuity, playthings, objects of art, and stores of wealth. Over the centuries, they've inspired the passion of mad kings, put miscreants behind bars, and provided story fodder for some of the world's greatest writers. In their functional role as "mere" timekeepers, they've lent invaluable help to science, industry and sports. And they've saved countless lives in myriad places: at sea, on the rails, in the cockpit, and on the battlefield.

This book is about the watch's many faces. It is, first of all, a piece of entertainment, a quiz show in print for watch fans who enjoy testing their knowledge of watches, in all their multifarious roles, and picking up new pieces of timepiece information. I hope it will serve a second purpose, a practical one, by providing useful information about watch technology, watch history, and the watch industry to those who, for professional reasons or simply out of curiosity, want to know more about the wide world of watches.

The book is written in question-and-answer format and divided into chapters dedicated to the many corners of our culture that watches inhabit: literature, painting, movies, the celebrity scene, crime, and so on. There are also chapters on watch technology, both mechanical and quartz, and how that technology evolved. The final chapter, "Odds and Ends," is devoted to leftover but nonetheless enticing watch tidbits that did not fit under any other rubric.

I gathered much of the information contained here during my 15 years of reporting on and writing about watches for trade and consumer magazines. Covering the watch beat has been a continuous delight to me, and one of its biggest joys has been unearthing little known but lively, and sometimes quirky, watch facts. In doing research for this project, I also read a wide range of watch books and articles, most of them listed in the "sources" section after the last chapter.

The idea for this book came from my husband, Joe Thompson, an acclaimed writer and reporter who has spent a quarter of a century covering the watch industry worldwide. He not only conceived the book, but fed it tirelessly, passing along to me barrels of fun facts from newspaper articles and history books and from his decades' worth of interviews with watch executives. I would never have started this project without him, nor would I ever have finished it, and I am deeply grateful to him for his help.

November 2005

PRESIDENTS AND PRIME MINISTERS

Which Rolex model is nicknamed the "President"?
The Day-Date. The watch, which was introduced in 1956, earned its sobriquet when Rolex gave one to Dwight Eisenhower. Today Rolex uses the name "President" to denote a particular bracelet style that features a hidden clasp.

For what president was the Bulova President named?
Calvin Coolidge. In 1924, Coolidge presented a Bulova watch to Stanley "Bucky" Harris, player for and manager of the Washington Senators, winners of that year's World Series. In honor of the event, Bulova designed a watch it named the "President."

During his first presidential campaign and first term in office, Bill Clinton was criticized in the press and by at least one Swiss watch company for wearing a watch its detractors deemed unworthy of high office. What watch was it?
A Timex Ironman Triathlon. Critics included *Washington Post* columnist Gene Weingarten, who derided

Clinton for wearing "a plastic digital watch, thick as a brick and handsome as a hernia." The Swiss watch company Omega, in a radio ad, suggested Clinton give up his Timex and don something more dignified.

In 1993 the watch company Valdawn brought out a character watch inspired by the Clinton presidency. What did it depict?
Socks, the Clintons' cat, playing a saxophone as two mice danced. Valdawn called the model the "First Cat" watch.

In 1994, Bill Clinton received as a gift a dress watch that he often wore in public. What watch was it and where did he get it?
It was a leather-strapped, analog watch from the French company Lip, given to him during his June trip to France for the commemoration of the 50th anniversary of D-Day. Charles de Gaulle and Dwight Eisenhower also owned Lip watches, prompting the company to dub its product "The Presidents' Watch."

During the Potsdam Conference, Harry Truman wore one of the most popular watches of the era. What was it?
A Universal Genève Tri-Compax. The watch, introduced in 1944, the year before Potsdam, featured a chronograph, calendar and moon-phase indicator. It was the most popular chronograph of the 1940s and '50s. Truman's watch, which was later engraved on the back, "Worn at Potsdam, July 1945 by Harry Truman," fetched 22,000 Swiss francs at an auction in 1994.

In August 1964 Lyndon Johnson appeared on the cover of _Newsweek_ magazine wearing what watch?
A Cricket given to him by the watch's manufacturer,

Vulcain & Studio, in La Chaux-de-Fonds, Switzerland. The Cricket, introduced in 1947, was named for the chirping sound of its alarm, which was considered the first wristwatch alarm loud enough to actually wake someone up. Johnson was apparently quite fond of the watch and wrote the company: "I value it highly and feel somewhat less than dressed without it." Presidents Eisenhower and Nixon also wore Crickets, which led to the manufacturer's nicknaming the model "The Presidents' Watch."

Richard Nixon owned a Vulcain Cricket. How did he get it?
It was given to him as a thank-you gift in 1955 when as vice president he addressed the National Association of Watch and Clock Makers. Nixon later wrote to Vulcain: "It has given excellent service over the past five years and has served as my alarm clock around the world."

What brand of watch was John F. Kennedy wearing when he was assassinated?
A Cartier. The watch was a gift from Jacqueline Kennedy on the couple's fourth wedding anniversary.

In 1962, the then governor of Pennsylvania, David Lawrence, gave John F. Kennedy a customized Hamilton watch. What was unusual about it?
The dial was photo-engraved with likenesses of JFK's two children, Caroline and John.

According to some political analysts, a watch helped Bill Clinton achieve his 1992 election victory over George H.W. Bush. How?
During the presidential debate on Oct. 15, 1992, Bush twice glanced at his watch, appearing to be bored with the proceedings. After the election,

pundits said some viewers might have interpreted the gesture as one of cavalier detachment and shunned Bush at the polls. Bush admitted he had been impatient for the debate to end. In a TV interview he asked rhetorically, "Was I glad the damn thing was over?" and recalled his thoughts as the debate was winding down: "Only 10 more minutes and I'll be done with this crap."

The watch George W. Bush wore during the 2000 presidential campaign reflected his taste for the straightforward; its manufacturer describes it as "the world's easiest to use alarm watch." What watch was it?
A Timex "i-Control" alarm watch. The wearer sets the alarm simply by turning the outer rim of the watch to the desired alarm time and pulling out a knob at 4 o'clock.

In 1788, George Washington asked Gouverneur Morris to buy a watch for him while Morris was in Europe. What watch did Morris get Washington?
One made by the famous French watchmaker Jean-Antoine Lépine. Washington's watch was a large, simple model with virgule escapement and Roman numerals.

Why did one U.S. president instruct an aide to "get rid of" a gold Rolex given to him for his birthday?
The president, John F. Kennedy, presumably feared that the watch, a gift from Marilyn Monroe, would be construed as evidence of an intimate relationship between them. Monroe gave Kennedy the watch for his 45th birthday (the same birthday on which she famously sang to him, "Happy Birthday, Mr. President"). The back of the watch was engraved, "Jack/

With love as always/from/Marilyn/May 29th 1962."
Monroe supposedly gave the watch to Kennedy aide
Kenneth O'Donnell to give to Kennedy. Instead of
accepting the watch, Kennedy told O'Donnell to "get
rid of" it. On Oct. 15, 2005, the Alexander Auto-
graphs auction house in Cos Cob, Connecticut, sold
the watch, along with a note describing Kennedy's
instructions to O'Donnell, an antique box that
contained the watch, and a love poem Monroe had
supposedly placed in the box, to a U.S. collector for
$120,000.

**In 1944, Franklin Delano Roosevelt wrote a letter
to the president of a watch company thanking him
for the gift of a marine chronometer that the man
had dropped off for him at the White House. What
company was it?**
Hamilton Watch Co. In his letter, FDR vowed: "For
the rest of the war I shall have it kept in the White
House map room and communication center…It will
be a helpful reminder to all of us what an important
factor accurate timekeeping is in the conduct of
modern warfare." Hamilton's extremely accurate
chronometers were vital to the U.S. war effort.

**Which U.S. president asked his wife for a particu-
lar digital watch for Christmas but was refused
because the watch was too expensive?**
Gerald Ford, who in 1974 asked his wife Betty for a
$4,000 Hamilton Pulsar calculator watch with light-
emitting-diode display. Ford already owned a simpler
Pulsar LED that he loved, wearing it most notably
while testifying at the 1974 Congressional hearings
on his pardon of Richard Nixon. The watch appeared
so prominently in a *Washington Post* photo that many
jewelers hung the picture in their stores to increase
Pulsar sales.

Former Israeli Prime Minister Ehud Barak wore a Breitling with an unusual feature. What was it?
His watch, a Chronomat, had what Breitling calls a "UTC auxiliary watch," a small, separate quartz watch that gives the time in a second time zone.

What future prime minister was advised by his father to buy "one of those cheap watches for 2 pounds as those are the only ones which if you smash are not very costly to replace"?
Winston Churchill. His father, Lord Randolph Churchill, was infuriated with the 19-year-old Winston for having, within just two weeks, twice broken a very valuable gold half-hunter watch he had given him. Winston, then a cadet at the Royal Military College at Sandhurst, wrote his father, attempting to pacify him. In the first mishap, he explained, he was entirely blameless: a boy running past him had accidentally knocked the watch out of his hand. He acknowledged more guilt in the second incident, in which he had dropped the watch into a 6-foot-deep pool of water as he was walking along a stream. He had tried to retrieve the watch by repeat-edly diving into the pool, he wrote. Those efforts failed, and he recovered the watch only by diverting the stream, with the help of 23 other men, and pumping the water from the pool. "I tell you all this to show you that I appreciated fully the value of the watch and that I did not treat the accident in a casual way," he wrote. Unconvinced, Lord Randolph gave the watch to Winston's brother, Jack, who kept it for the rest of his life. That Lord Randolph learned of Winston's watch mishaps at all was due only to a stroke of bad luck: Lord Randolph happened to take his own watch to the same watchmaker, at the famous London firm E. Dent & Co., who was at that very time repairing Winston's watch after its deep dive.

Winston Churchill appears in a print advertisement for what watch brand?
Breguet. The advertisement shows a photo of a somber-faced Churchill in homburg and overcoat. The copy reads, "Sir Winston Churchill, from 1901, a client of Breguet's."

The Smithsonian Institution's National Museum of American History has in its collections an Ellery model Waltham pocket watch owned by which president?
Abraham Lincoln. The watch is a key-wound, 11-jewel, 18-size model made in 1863. The Ellery watch, an economical model designed for use by Civil War soldiers, was a great success for Waltham, accounting for nearly half of the company's unit sales and one-third of its dollar volume in 1865, the year the war ended.

Which U.S. president was at one time so poor that he pawned his pocket watch, most likely so that he could buy Christmas presents for his family?
Ulysses S. Grant. Just before Christmas 1857, after Grant had temporarily left the army and was trying to scrape out a living as a farmer near St. Louis, he pawned his gold hunting watch for $22, probably to buy presents for his wife and three children.

TIME FLIES

What watch is called the "moon watch"?
The Omega Speedmaster. It is so nicknamed because NASA chose it as the official watch of the Apollo moon missions.

Who was the first man to wear a watch on the moon?
Edwin "Buzz" Aldrin. He wore an Omega Speedmaster, issued by NASA, when he stepped onto the moon on July 21, 1969, during the historic Apollo XI mission.

When Neil Armstrong took man's first step onto the moon during the Apollo XI mission, he left his watch behind in the lunar module. Why?
The module's clock had stopped, and Armstrong left behind his watch, an Omega Speedmaster, as a backup. Fourteen minutes later, Edwin "Buzz" Aldrin stepped onto the moon's surface wearing his own Omega Speedmaster.

Although NASA in 1965 chose the Omega Speed-master for use on space missions, many NASA

astronauts continued to sport Rolexes, long a favorite of aviators. Which Rolex model did they wear most often?

The GMT Master, so named because its additional hour hand, used in conjunction with its rotating bezel, gives Greenwich Mean Time (or the time in any time zone the wearer chooses).

What inspired Rolex to launch the GMT Master?

The growing popularity of intercontinental air travel in the 1950s. The watch was developed for airline pilots so they could keep track of both local time and the time at home.

If not for an error by a Rolex employee, the first watch worn on the moon might have been a Rolex. What was the mistake?

Refusing to send NASA the chronographs it requested so it could test them for possible use by its astronauts. When NASA phoned Rolex USA to ask for 50 watches, the Rolex employee who took the call replied dismissively that the company could not send them because it did not have enough watches available. Rolex later expressed regret at the cavalier way in which NASA's request had been handled.

A Cartier watch still in production today was inspired a century ago by an aviator. What watch is it?

The Santos. In the first years of the 20th century, the then-renowned Brazilian airship and airplane pilot Alberto Santos-Dumont asked Louis Cartier, grandson of the founder of the Cartier jewelry firm, to make him a wristwatch. The pilot reasoned that such a watch would be easier to use while he was flying than the pocket watches preferred by nearly everyone at the time. This watch, of which no record remains (the Cartier company says it made the watch around 1904), became the inspiration a few years later for a square-cased model with distinctive screws around the bezel and a movement made by Edmond Jaeger. This watch was called the "Santos-Dumont." The first reference to such a model by name appears in the Cartier archives from 1913. (A sketch of a square case like the one used in the Santos-Dumont dates to 1911, but no name appears on the drawing.) The company later shortened the name to "Santos."

What watch did Chuck Yeager wear in October 1947 when he became the first pilot to break the sound barrier?
A Rolex Oyster. Later on, Yeager's appreciation of Rolex watches inspired the company to feature the world-renowned pilot in its print advertisements.

Who designed the Longines Hour Angle watch?
Charles Lindbergh. He designed it as an aid for pilots navigating by celestial observation. It was introduced in 1931.

To what does the term "hour angle," as used in the name of the Longines Hour Angle watch, refer?
The distance west, expressed in hours, minutes and seconds, of the sun or a star from a particular celestial meridian. This distance is used in celestial navigation. The Hour Angle watch enabled the wearer to read the Greenwich hour angle–the distance of the sun or a star from the Greenwich meridian–directly off the watch by means of a graduated rotating ring on the dial. It obviated many laborious pencil-and-paper calculations.

The design of the Longines Hour Angle watch was based on another watch. Which one?

The Longines Second Setting watch, designed by the famous navigation expert Philip Van Horn Weems. The watch, which was first manufactured in 1929, had an interior rotating dial that enabled the wearer to synchronize the watch precisely to a radio time signal. When Charles Lindbergh designed the Hour Angle, he incorporated this feature into it, and added the graduated rotating hour angle ring that gave the watch its name. The U.S. Air Corps issued Weems's Second Setting watch to pilots between 1932 and 1943.

In the late 1960s, astronauts Walter Schirra and Eugene Cernan wore, on the Apollo VII and Apollo X missions respectively, a watch that had become a symbol of American culture. Which watch was it?
A Mickey Mouse watch.

The history of the German watch company Tutima contains a notable aviation-related "first." What was it?
In 1941 the company produced the first German-made wrist chronographs for the Luftwaffe.

The Milestones of Flight exhibit in the Smithsonian Institution's National Air and Space Museum contains an object bearing the name of the Breitling watch brand. What object is it?
The gondola of the Breitling Orbiter 3, which in 1999 became the first manned balloon in history to circle the earth without stopping. Bertrand Piccard and Brian Jones were its pilots. Breitling sponsored the flight, and both the balloon and the 18-by-10-foot, 4,400-pound gondola that is on display at the Smithsonian are emblazoned with the company's name.

Why did the U.S. government ask Bulova to delay the introduction of its Accutron wristwatch?

The government didn't want the Soviet Union to get its hands on Bulova's revolutionary new Accutron movement sooner than was absolutely necessary. The movement's tuning-fork oscillator made it the most accurate watch movement then in existence. NASA planned to use Accutron timers on its satellites, and knew that introducing the Accutron watch before the first Accutron-timed satellite was launched would be tipping its hand to the Soviets. Bulova therefore agreed to delay the watch's introduction until after the launch of the first Accutron-timed satellite, the Explorer VI, in July 1960. The Accutron wristwatch came out four months later.

Following his failed attempt in 1933 to set a world's record for flying around the world, James "Jimmie" Mattern wrote a letter to A. Wittnauer Co. Why?

To congratulate the company on the durability and accuracy of its All-Proof watch, which Mattern had worn during his attempt to make a solo flight around the world. Mattern's mission had failed: he was forced to crash-land in Siberia when his plane began to leak oil. His All-Proof, however, proved invincible. After the ordeal, he wrote Wittnauer that the watch had survived not just the hard landing but also the days-long trek that followed, one that entailed swimming across rivers. "It personifies mechanical perfection heretofore unknown to me," he wrote. Others were impressed with it as well, he pointed out: "It was a sensation with the Eskimos in Anadyr [Siberia] who considered it something super-natural."

AOPA (the Aircraft Owners and Pilots Association) chose the Breitling Navitimer as its official watch soon after the timepiece was launched in 1952. What special feature made it suitable for pilots?

Then as now, the Navitimer was equipped with a circular built-in slide rule that enabled pilots to make such calculations as distance conversions, ascent and descent rates, fuel consumption and average speed. The slide rule consisted of a rotating bezel marked with numeric scales, which were used in conjunction with a fixed scale around the edge of the watch dial. Breitling first used the circular slide-rule concept for its Chronomat watch, introduced in 1942. (Today's Chronomats do not have slide rules.)

A former astronaut was once chairman of what watch company?

Omega Watch Corp., the U.S. branch of Omega SA in Switzerland. Thomas Stafford, a retired Air Force lieutenant general, was named to the post in 1980. Stafford flew aboard Gemini VI and was commander of Gemini IX, Apollo X and Apollo XVIII, the mission that in 1975 performed the historic rendezvous with the Soviet craft Soyuz. He was also head of the NASA Astronaut Office, supervising the day-to-day work of all NASA astronauts on the Apollo XII through Apollo XVII missions, and served as NASA's deputy director of flight crew operations. Stafford is now a member of the executive board of the Swatch Group U.S., the American subsidiary of the Swatch Group SA, which owns the Omega brand.

In 1956 Citizen staged a series of demonstrations to show how shock-resistant its Parashock watch was. What did the demonstrations consist of?

Citizen dropped the watch from a helicopter at various locations around Japan, including baseball fields and the Kyoto train station. The Parashock always kept ticking.

Vacheron Constantin claims that one of its watches

was worn during a groundbreaking flight in the early days of aviation. What flight was it?

The Wright brothers' flight–the first airplane flight in history–at Kitty Hawk on Dec. 17, 1903. The company refers to the watch on its website: "It was not by chance that the Wright brothers chose to wear a watch [during the famous flight] housing a caliber by Vacheron Constantin. The watch is now part of watch history." It is a pocket watch with steel case, enamel dial and red hands. Lugs were added to the watch, and, like some later pilots' watches, it has a leather strap long enough so the watch can be worn around one's thigh or over a jacket sleeve.

Admiral Richard Byrd was assisted in his famous second expedition over Antarctica by roughly 50 timepieces made by one company. Which one?

Longines. On the expedition, which took place between 1933 and 1935, Byrd used some 50 Longines chronographs, chronometers and wrist-watches for navigation and scientific observations.

When Scandinavian Airlines (SAS) flew over the North Pole in 1954, thus inaugurating the airline's polar route to North America, crew members wore a wristwatch named for the new shortcut. Which watch was it?

The Polerouter by Universal Genève. The watch, an automatic, was designed to withstand the strong magnetic fields of the Pole.

What watch executive wrote a book entitled *Man's Fight to Fly*?

John P.V. Heinmuller, president of Longines-Wittnauer. Heinmuller was an aviation expert and served as chief timer for the National Aeronautic Association. He timed several famous flights, including Charles Lindbergh's 1927 crossing of the Atlantic. He developed many aviation instruments and navigational timepieces, often with advice from prominent aviators like Lindbergh and Admiral Richard Byrd. In his book, published in 1944, he wrote about notable flights in the early days of aviation, including many he had witnessed himself.

What is the Snoopy Award, which Omega received in 1970?

An award given by NASA to employees and NASA contractors who have played especially important roles in the agency's space missions. NASA gave the award to Omega "for dedication, professionalism, and outstanding contributions in support of the first United States manned lunar landing project Apollo." The Omega Speedmaster was the official watch of the Apollo missions.

What pilot wrote a book that includes an affectionate description of a watch given to him by his grandfather?

Charles Lindbergh. In *The Spirit of St. Louis*, an account of his famous flight over the Atlantic in 1927, Lindbergh writes the following: "I hold the watch in my palm for a moment. It always stirs old memories...we've passed through many an interesting hour together. We've spilled off my motorcycle, stunted in my planes, made–let's see–eighteen parachute jumps all told; and now we've flown across an ocean." Lindbergh ends the reverie by praising the watch, never identified by brand, for always being accurate, "unmindful of the changing time and space through which it passes." *The Spirit of St. Louis*, published in 1953, won a Pulitzer Prize.

ON SCREENS
LARGE AND SMALL

The world's first TV commercial was for a watch brand. Which one?
Bulova. The ad, which aired July 1, 1941, showed an outline of a map of the United States. In its center was a watch dial labeled "Bulova Watch Time." The image remained onscreen for 20 seconds while a voice announced the time. The commercial was aired by WNBT during a Brooklyn Dodgers-Philadelphia Phillies baseball game at Ebbets Field.

In what movie does a character played by Tallulah Bankhead own a watch she refers to as a "Philip Pateek"?
Alfred Hitchcock's *Lifeboat* (1944). The watch is incorporated into a cigarette lighter. Bankhead's character, a hard-boiled newspaper reporter named Constance Porter, haughtily defends her watch's accuracy while adrift in a lifeboat with other survivors of a German torpedo attack. "What time is it?" asks one of her companions. "Ten past seven," she replies, looking at the lighter. "I think you're slow," says the other character. "Slow?! That's a Philip Pateek!" she exclaims indignantly.

In 1975, Girard-Perregaux introduced a watch bearing the name of what movie?
The Graduate, released in 1967. The watch was named after the Italian translation of the title, *Il Laureato*. In Italy, it became a popular graduation gift. The Laureato is still being produced today in an updated version.

What chain-smoking author, director and TV host sometimes wore a Hamilton Ventura on the air?
Rod Serling, host of *The Twilight Zone*, which aired from 1959 to 1964. He can be seen wearing the watch during his introductions to some episodes of the show.

Who wore a Hamilton Ventura in his role as a soldier-turned-tour-guide in a 1961 film?
Elvis Presley. He wears the black-dial version of the watch, introduced in 1957, in several scenes of the movie *Blue Hawaii*.

In 1933, the Waterbury Clock Co. launched a watch through a licensing agreement with a Hollywood, California-based company. What watch was it?
The Mickey Mouse watch. Waterbury introduced the watch at the World's Fair in Chicago, where it sold for $2.95. The company marketed the Mickey Mouse under the brand name Ingersoll, which it had ac- quired in 1922 when it bought the bankrupt Robert H. Ingersoll & Bro. watch firm. The watch was a fabulous success, selling in the millions.

One version of the Rolex Cosmograph Daytona has been nicknamed the "Paul Newman." Why?
One oft-heard explanation is that Newman wore the watch in his role as a race-car driver in the 1969

movie *Winning*. Another is that he wore it in a photo on the cover of an Italian magazine. Which of these is correct (if either) is unclear. (Rolex itself does not use the name "Paul Newman" to describe the watch.)

How is the "Paul Newman" Rolex Cosmograph Daytona different from other Cosmograph Daytona models?

The constant-seconds subdial on the "Paul Newman" has numerals at the 15-, 30-, 45- and 60-second positions. Other Daytonas have them at the 20-, 40- and 60-second spots. In addition, the markers on all the "Paul Newman" subdials are decorated with square tips, while those on other Daytonas are simple, straight lines.

On his hit sitcom, Jerry Seinfeld often wore watches from which watch brand?

Breitling. In real life, Seinfeld is a big Breitling fan, and has made personal appearances on behalf of the brand.

In what movie does a character played by Bruce Willis risk his life for a gold wristwatch?

Pulp Fiction (1994). The watch has been passed down to Willis's character, a washed-up prizefighter named Butch Coolidge, by his great-grandfather. It has survived World Wars I and II and the Vietnam War, during which Coolidge's father died in a POW camp. Coolidge cherishes the watch for its sentimental value. He risks being killed by petty gangsters when he retrieves it from his apartment, where his girlfriend has accidentally left it. A character named Captain Koons, played by Christopher Walken, says the watch was "made by the first company to ever make wrist-watches." No brand name is discernible on the watch.

In the late 1960s, the Heuer watch brand (precur-

sor to today's **TAG Heuer**) got a big promotional boost through its association with a TV show. What show was it?

60 Minutes. The stopwatch shown during the introduction was a Heuer model; its name was clearly visible on the watch face. In the show's early days (it first aired in 1968) many viewers called the network to find out where they could buy the watch and were sent a free Heuer stopwatch as a reward for tuning in. Eventually, the network replaced the Heuer with a cheaper watch that made the watch giveaway policy less costly.

In several scenes of his last movie, the 1926 silent classic *Son of the Sheik*, Rudolph Valentino wears a wristwatch. What watch is it?

A Cartier Tank. Valentino insisted on wearing it despite its being markedly out of place on the wrist of his character, a swaggering Arab sheik (Valentino actually played two sheiks in the movie, a father and son).

Which James Bond movie includes a prominent shot of a Seiko billboard and features a Seiko watch loaded with explosives?

Moonraker (1979). In it, Roger Moore's Bond, riding in an ambulance, passes a billboard advertising two Seiko watches, an analog and a digital. Later, he opens the back of his own digital Seiko and uses the explosives hidden there to blast through a door and escape death.

In what movie does James Bond use his watch to try to find some atomic bombs?

Thunderball (1965). The watch, a Breitling Top Time, is equipped with a Geiger counter. Bond, played by Sean Connery, wears the watch while scuba diving in search of two atomic bombs in the possession of the enemy organization SPECTRE.

In the James Bond movie *GoldenEye* (1995), what life-saving feature does the hero's watch possess?
A laser beam that allows him to cut through metal and escape from the train where his enemies, members of Russian organized crime, are holding him captive. The watch is an Omega Seamaster. Pierce Brosnan plays James Bond.

In *Live and Let Die*, (1973) the Rolex Submariner worn by Roger Moore's James Bond has two special features. What are they?
A "hyper-intensified magnetic field" (as Bond describes it) that can be activated by pushing a button (or, in one scene, turning the bezel), and a bezel that can double as a saw. Bond uses the magnet to unzip the dress of one of his conquests and, later, to pick up the gas-filled pellet that kills the movie's villain. The saw feature comes into play when Bond needs to cut through ropes that bind him and his fellow captive, played by Jane Seymour. The actual prop used in the movie–a souped-up case with no movement–was sold at auction in 2004 for 26,523 pounds sterling (including sales commission). Renderings of the watch sold at the same sale for 7,233 pounds.

One night on the *Tonight Show*, host Johnny Carson showed the audience a watch that was new on the market and getting much press attention. He then threw it over his shoulder and declared contemptuously that it would "never put Mickey Mouse out of business." What watch was it?
A Hamilton Pulsar, the world's first digital watch, which had a light-emitting-diode (LED) display that lit up at the push of a button. Introduced in 1972,

the Pulsar became an instant star, as famous as the people who wore it, who included the Shah of Iran, Sammy Davis Jr., Gerald Ford, Richard Nixon, and many others.

What now-celebrated series of watch commercials debuted on Steve Allen's variety show?
Timex's "torture test" commercials, in which Timex watches were subjected to a variety of abuses in order to prove their durability. Ex-newsman John Cameron Swayze hosted the spots, which debuted in 1958. Allen's show aired on NBC on Sunday nights from 8 to 9 Eastern Standard Time.

A famous mishap occurred during one of the early Timex "torture test" spots, which were broadcast live. What was it?
The test called for a Timex to be strapped to the blade of an outboard motor, which was placed in a tank of water and turned on. When the motor was stopped, viewers saw that the watch had fallen off the blade and was lying on the bottom of the tank. Timex spokesman John Cameron Swayze apologized to viewers and assured them they would see the demonstration performed successfully the following week. They did.

In 1967, movie director Stanley Kubrick visited the Hamilton Watch Co. in Lancaster, Pennsylvania. Why?
He wanted the company to make a prop, an avant-garde digital clock, for his upcoming movie, *2001: A Space Odyssey*. (With him was science fiction writer Arthur C. Clarke, who wrote the book on which the movie was based.) Hamilton obliged. The clock was a prototype of sorts for the company's Pulsar watch, the world's first digital watch, which was put on the market in 1972.

In the 1920s, Movado introduced a watch named after what dead movie star?
Rudolph Valentino. The company introduced two versions of the "Valentino" watch, a pocket watch and a wristwatch, soon after the star's death in 1926 at age 31. Both watches had cases that could be covered with leather (extant examples are covered in snakeskin).

One actor was so fond of the watch he wore in the 1996 movie *Daylight* that he asked the watch's manufacturer to make him 400 more to give to friends and colleagues. Who was the actor and what watch was it?
The actor was Sylvester Stallone, who played the movie's hero, and the watch a Panerai Mare Nostrum. Each watch bore the words "Panerai Slytech" on the dial and Stallone's signature on the case back.

Which company launched a watch-cum-TV in 1983?
Seiko. The watch, which was battery-powered, had a 1.2-inch screen and a radio, time display, chronograph and alarm. It came with earphones and a tuner and retailed for $435. It was on the market just 18 months before technical problems and slow sales brought its fadeout.

Which company in the 1990s used in its commercials the statement, "More people depend on a watch made by _____ than any other timepiece on earth"?
Citizen. The company based its claim to world dominance on the fact that it made more watch movements than any other company.

What company proclaimed in its ads, "…more people buy _____ than any other watch in the world"?

Timex. The company started using the slogan in 1958 after a tremendous growth surge. In 1959, the company claimed that one-quarter of all watches sold in the United States were Timex models. The spurt continued through the 1960s. By 1967, Timex was claiming a 50% market share in the United States.

In the 1950s, one watch company sponsored a late-night TV show featuring journalists interviewing prominent newsmakers. What show was it?
The Longines Chronoscope. The show aired on CBS from 1951 to 1955. Its producer and director was Alan Cartoun, son of Fred Cartoun, head of the Longines-Wittnauer Watch Co. The show's many famous guests included Senator Joseph McCarthy, Clare Booth Luce and John F. Kennedy. Each program ended with a Longines-Wittnauer commercial narrated by *Chronoscope* host Frank Knight.

In what 1950 movie does a father keep his large family in line by timing their every move with a stopwatch?
Cheaper by the Dozen, starring Clifton Webb and Myrna Loy. The movie was inspired by real-life efficiency experts Frank and Lillian Gilbreth and their 12 children.

Bob Hope appeared as a TV spokesman for Timex in the late 1950s until the company dismissed him. Why was he fired?
Because he had appeared on a TV show sponsored by Timex's rival, Bulova.

What watch does Jimmy Stewart wear in Alfred Hitchcock's *Rear Window* (1954)?
A plain, round Tissot. Hitchcock shows a close-up of the watch when the photographer/hero played by

Stewart checks the time while observing the salesman/ murderer played by Raymond Burr leaving his apartment carrying a part or parts of his wife's body in his sample case.

In the movie *Marathon Man*, (1976) how does the hero's Rolex help him out of an awkward situation?
The hero, played by Dustin Hoffman, gives it to a taxi driver as payment for a ride and some coins to make a phone call. Hoffman, who is being pursued by his foes, has no money with him and can't pay the driver except with the watch, which is a gift from his brother.

What actor wore a Heuer Monaco in the 1971 movie *Le Mans*?
Steve McQueen. He plays a race-car driver who recovers from a serious accident to compete in the famous Le Mans race in France.

WATCHES AND WAR

What famous American general became chairman of Bulova?

World War II hero Omar Bradley. As head of the Veterans Administration after the war, Bradley came into contact with Bulova through the Joseph Bulova School, which Bulova chief Arde Bulova had founded in 1944 to teach watchmaking to disabled veterans. (The school was named after Arde Bulova's father, the founder of Bulova.) Bradley joined Bulova Watch Co. in 1953. He retired from his daily duties in 1973 but stayed on as honorary chairman and a consultant. He died in 1981.

Why did U.S. pilots bomb International Watch Co. of Schaffhausen (IWC) during World War II?

It was an accident. Believing they were over German territory, U.S. pilots mistakenly bombed the Swiss town of Schaffhausen, very near the Swiss-German border. Forty-five people were killed. One bomb hit the IWC factory but did not detonate. Fire from a neighboring building that had been bombed spread to the factory but the flames were extinguished before they destroyed it.

Seiko's popularity in the United States got a major boost due to what war?

The Vietnam War. Many U.S. soldiers bought Seiko watches while in the Far East. The brand's popularity stateside grew by word-of-mouth recommendations when the GI's returned home.

Which war is credited with popularizing the wristwatch?

World War I. Although wristwatches played a role in earlier wars, it was not until the Great War that large numbers of soldiers from many countries first wore them. When the soldiers returned home, the trend spread to civilians. Until then, most men had rejected the new timepieces as effeminate (a few fashion-conscious women were sporting them as early as the turn of the century).

What company began making watches as a result of a war?

Panerai. The company produced its first watch, a prototype of a divers' watch, in 1936 at the request of the Italian Navy during Italy's war with Ethiopia. Italy had invaded that country and as a result was being threatened by the British fleet in the Mediterranean. The Italian Navy had no battleships. It knew it would have to rely on underwater commando operations to fight the British, and would therefore need divers' watches. The navy turned to Panerai, which was already supplying it with other military instruments, to make them. As it turned out, Italy conquered Ethiopia in the spring of 1936 and tensions with Britain subsided. Production of the divers' watches was put on hold. It was only in 1938, when war loomed once again, that Panerai began series production of the watches (which contained Rolex movements). The watch was later christened the Radiomir, its name inspired by the radium that made the watches' markers glow in the dark.

The development of the self-winding wristwatch was closely linked to World War I. How?

The first self-winding, or automatic, wristwatch to make use of the winding-rotor system we know today was the work of a World War I British soldier named John Harwood. While fighting in the trenches, he saw that dirt and dust often wreaked havoc on watch movements, and reasoned that one way to keep dirt out would be to eliminate the winding-crown hole through which most of the dirt entered the watch case. Using a concept invented in the 18th century, he devised a watch that did not need a winding crown because it wound itself automatically by means of a weight that swung in response to the motions of the wearer's arm. Harwood's watch failed commercially for both technical and aesthetic reasons, but it did lay the foundation–the swinging-rotor concept–on which Rolex created the first truly successful self-winding watch, the Perpetual, in 1933. The winding-rotor system is now used in all automatic watches.

What was the purpose of a "hacking" device, a feature of many mechanical military wristwatches?

It enabled soldiers to synchronize their watches. A hacking device stopped the watch's seconds hand when the soldier pulled the watch's winding stem out to the setting position. Typically, he would stop the hand at 12 o'clock, then set the minutes and hours hands to the agreed-upon time and restart the movement by pushing the stem back in.

World War II gave the Swiss watch industry a big boost. How?

During the war, the watch industries of the United

States, Japan and Germany shifted from making civilian watches to making war materiel, including military wristwatches. The Swiss industry stepped in to meet consumer demand for civilian wristwatches, thus increasing its lead as the world's most important watch producer. That lead solidified further after the war, when the watch industries of the former combatants had to spend time converting back to civilian-watch production, thus giving the Swiss a jump in meeting the post-war boom in consumer demand.

Just before World War II interrupted Japanese watch production, the country's output exceeded 5 million watches per year. How long did it take Japan's watch factories to reach that level of production again?
20 years.

Cartier named one of its most famous watch styles after a piece of war apparatus. What watch was it?
The Tank. The watch was named for its resemblance, when viewed from the side, to the treads of a military tank. When the watch was introduced, in 1919, the military tank was a new and headline-grabbing invention, having first been used in battle in 1916 in France.

One World War I figure, whose wartime adventures were the basis of a movie, was an early wristwatch wearer, sporting an Omega single-button chronograph well before wristwatches became popular. Who was it?
Lawrence of Arabia. Omega made the watch in 1912 and Lawrence (a k a T.E. Shaw) owned it until his death in 1935. In 2000, Omega repurchased the watch at auction for 86,000 Swiss francs.

Mere hours before World War II ended in Europe,

the main factory of one watch company was almost completely destroyed by Russian bombs. What company was it?

A. Lange & Söhne, in Glashütte, Germany. The bombing was just the start of the company's woes: 3 years later the new Communist government confiscated it. It was not until after German reunification in 1990 that A. Lange & Söhne was re-established.

The military watches of World War I sometimes posed a hazard to those who made them. What was it?

Radiation sickness. Many of the watches had markers and hands made luminous by a coating of radium. Some of the workers who painted the radium onto the watches developed radiation sickness because of their close contact with the substance, especially their practice of licking the tips of their paintbrushes to sharpen the points. After the war, luminous watch dials became a fad with consumers. In the 1920s, knowledge of the plight of the dial painters became public due to a liability lawsuit filed by a group of employees, dubbed the "Radium Girls," against the U.S. Radium Corp.

In one of the earliest efforts at promoting wristwatches, British jewelers used testimonials from soldiers returning from what war?

The Boer War (1899-1902), the first war in which a significant number of soldiers wore wristwatches. Because it was relatively small in scope, the Boer War did not spark a vogue for wristwatch-wearing the way World War I did later.

The first series-produced wristwatches are believed to have been produced in the 19th century for German naval officers. Who made them?

Girard-Perregaux. In 1879 Kaiser Wilhelm I ordered 2,000 of the company's watches for the officers and took delivery of them the following year. The watches had protective metal grids over their crystals. The company tried to introduce the watches in other markets but was unable to elicit interest in them.

What was "It's Time You Knew"?
An illustrated, quiz-style, recurring feature that Bulova Watch Co. wrote and placed in more than 400 newspapers during World War II. The feature consisted of questions and answers about war, history, movie stars, natural wonders, Bulova, and watches in general.

Shortly after World War II, two U.S. generals, Dwight Eisenhower and Carl Spaatz, each bought the same watch. What watch was it?
A wrist chronograph (reference 2447) by Heuer (forerunner of today's TAG Heuer).

The Duke of Wellington bought himself a Breguet watch to celebrate what military victory?
His defeat of Napoleon at the Battle of Waterloo in June 1815. Three weeks after the battle, he went to Paris, where he treated himself to a Breguet montre à tact, designed to be read by touch in the dark. Wellington had bought his first Breguet watch a few months earlier. He purchased many more Breguet timepieces before his death in 1852.

How did watches save the lives of scores of Jews held in concentration camps during World War II?
The concentration camp at Sachsenhausen, Germany, contained a watchmaking workshop to which some 160 Jewish watchmakers were transferred from other camps, including Auschwitz, to repair watches

confiscated from fellow prisoners. The watchmakers received better treatment than the other prisoners and most survived. The Germans used the watches primarily as gifts for German officers and soldiers and for civilians who helped in the war effort.

One Christmastime advertisement for Ingersoll watches showed a photo of a bomb-fuse timer sitting in an Ingersoll watch box underneath a Christmas tree. What was the point of the ad?
That the company had shifted to making materiel, especially timing devices for bombs, for the U.S. effort in World War II and was therefore not selling any civilian watches. The ad copy read, "We're sorry…this Christmas Season must find us making things for destruction instead of gifts of good will… We are making Ingersoll watches now, of course, but they are hardly suitable for gift-giving. For these 'watches' ride in the noses of ack-ack shells to release deadly explosives in sky-paths of the enemy…"

What watch did Lord Nelson have with him when he died in the Battle of Trafalgar in 1805?
A gold watch made by the famous Swiss-born, London-based watchmaker Josiah Emery around 1787. Emery was celebrated as only the second watchmaker, after Thomas Mudge, to make a watch with a lever escapement, now used almost universally in the watch industry. He made about 36 lever-escapement watches, including Nelson's. It was to have been auctioned off by Sotheby's on Oct. 5, 2005 at a sale of Nelson-related items, but was instead bought, for an undisclosed sum, by U.S. businessman Bruce McMahan about a month before the sale. Sotheby's had estimated the watch would bring between 250,000 and 350,000 pounds (about $430,000 to $600,000). Nelson probably paid about

100 pounds (the equivalent today of about 10,000 pounds) for it.

A watch nicknamed the "Victory Watch" sold at auction for nearly $700,000 in 2005. What military hero once owned it?

Lord Nelson. The watch was auctioned off by Sotheby's in London on Oct. 5, 2005 at a sale of Nelson-related items. The watch, an alarm model, was made by the prominent London watchmaker James McCabe. It bears the inscription: "Pres. to Adml. Lord Nelson By the Officers of HMS Victory Aug. 20, 1805." The officers gave him the watch to mark the end of their tour of duty. He owned it for just two months. On Oct. 21, 1805, Nelson, sailing on the HMS Victory, directed British forces during the Battle of Trafalgar, the greatest naval triumph in British history, and died from a bullet wound incurred during the battle. The watch sold for 400,000 pounds (about $690,000).

DRIVE TIME

What watch company executive is a former professional race-car driver and owner of some 50 racing cars?
Luigi (better known as Gino) Macaluso, owner of Girard-Perregaux. In 1972 Macaluso won the European Rally Championship in a Fiat 124 Abarth. He quit professional racing in 1975 but remains an ardent racing enthusiast and automobile collector. He bought Girard-Perregaux in 1992.

Since 1994, two watch companies have made deals with the Ferrari car company to market watches under the Ferrari name. What companies are they?
Girard-Perregaux and Panerai. The former signed an agreement in 1994 to market watches under the "pour Ferrari" label. In 2005, at the expiration of the G-P contract, Panerai signed on with the company and is scheduled to introduce its Ferrari watch collection in the spring of 2006.

What is a tachymeter?
A numerical scale on the periphery of a watch dial that, when used in conjunction with a chronograph,

indicates average speed over a pre-measured distance. The wearer starts the chronograph at the beginning of the measured distance, typically a full mile or kilometer, stops it at the end, and reads his or her average speed, in miles or kilometers per hour, off the tachymeter scale.

The Swatch Group was once part of a joint venture that developed what car?
The Smart car, nicknamed the "Swatchmobile." In 1994, the watch company (then known as SMH), joined with Daimler-Benz (now DaimlerChrysler), to form a joint venture to develop the Smart car, an 8-foot-long mini-car designed for city driving. It was introduced in 1998. The Swatch Group sold its share in the venture to Daimler-Benz in November of that year.

What auto magnate repaired watches as a teenager and considered starting a watch business himself?
Henry Ford. In the early 1880s, he worked evenings cleaning and repairing watches for a Detroit jeweler named Robert Magill. He earned 50 cents a night, which supplemented the 2 dollars a week paid him for his day job at the Detroit Dry Dock Co. Ford toyed with the idea of going into the watch business himself, but was doubtful he could sell enough watches to make a decent profit.

What company was the official timer for Formula 1 racing from 1992 to 2003?
TAG Heuer. The company is now the official timer for Indy Racing League racing and the Indianapolis 500. TAG Heuer is also a sponsor and official timekeeper for the Formula 1 team West McLaren Mercedes.

In 1994, TAG Heuer introduced a watch named

after what dead race-car driver?

Ayrton Senna. Before his death on May 1, 1994, following a crash at the San Marino Grand Prix, the three-time Formula 1 world champion Senna had signed a contract with TAG Heuer to launch a watch bearing his name. In October 1994, TAG reached an agreement with the Senna Foundation to launch a commemorative Senna watch as part of the watch company's 6000 series. For each watch sold, TAG contributed 500 Swiss francs to the foundation for its charitable activities.

What car race lent its name to a collection of men's watches by Chopard?

The Mille Miglia, a 1,000-mile vintage-car race held in Italy. ("Mille miglia" is Italian for "1,000 miles.") The route runs from Brescia, in the north of the country, south to Rome and back. The first Mille Miglia took place in 1927.

The famous Breguet watch collector Sir David Lionel Salomons also loved cars. What auto-related "first" is he known for?

Organizing, in 1895, the first automobile show in England. It took place in Tunbridge Wells, southeast of London, where Salomons was mayor. Salomons was an extremely accomplished mechanic and electrical engineer (when he wired his house in 1874, it became England's first private residence with electricity) and was fascinated by all types of machines. He designed cars and, before that, a motorized tricycle, which a law forbade him from riding unless someone on foot carrying a red flag preceded him. (Salomons fought to have such restrictions on motor travel rescinded.) His enthusiasm for the watches of Abraham-Louis Breguet and the firm he founded matched his passion for cars; he was one of the biggest Breguet collectors in history. His Breguets included the celebrated Marie Antoinette, the most complicated watch of its time (it was completed in 1827, 44 years after one of Marie Antoinette's admirers had commissioned it for her). That watch and many other Breguets once owned by Salomons were stolen from a museum in Jerusalem in 1983.

What is a drivers' watch?
A watch with a sharply curved case designed to be worn on the side of the wrist so a driver can see the dial without having to take his or her hand off the wheel. Gruen and Hamilton made such watches in the late 1930s and early 1940s.

What watch brand does car-racing legend Michael Schumacher endorse?
Omega. The six-time Formula 1 world champion has been promoting the Omega Speedmaster since 1996.

What watch brand does Michael Schumacher's brother, Ralf, endorse?
Oris. Schumacher, a driver on the BMW Williams Formula 1 Team, began promoting Oris in 2004.

In 1964, Heuer introduced a watch named after a car race that had been discontinued because it was so dangerous. What watch was it?
The Carrera. The race was the Carrera Panamericana Mexico, which originated as a promotional event for the Pan-American Highway, the Mexican segment of which was completed in 1950. The course, which was 3,100 kilometers long and reached from one end of Mexico to the other, was both thrilling and perilous, incorporating plunging gorges, steep mountains, and hairpin turns. The race was run five times, from 1950

though 1954, but was discontinued due to the many accidents that occurred during it. It was resurrected in 1988.

What car-company founder owned the most complicated watch of its time?

James Ward Packard, founder of the Packard Motor Car Co. He was a devoted Patek Philippe collector, commissioning some 13 complicated watches from the company between 1905 and 1927. The last came to be known as "The Packard," and was for a few years the most complicated watch in the world. It had a perpetual calendar, repeater, indicators for rising and setting times of the sun, the solar hour and the phase of the moon. Its most unusual feature was a rotating disk that showed the position of the stars as seen from Packard's home in Ohio. The auto magnate bought the watch in 1927 for $16,000. In 1933, the financier Henry Graves Jr., also a Patek collector, ordered an even more complicated watch from the company, paying $75,000.

What was the "crash" watch?

A watch introduced in the 1960s by Cartier. Its name came from the fact that the watch was misshapen and hence looked as if it had been in a car wreck.

Both TAG Heuer and Parmigiani Fleurier have unveiled watches whose radically unorthodox movements were inspired by car engines. What watches are they?

The TAG Heuer Monaco V4 Concept Watch and the Parmigiani Bugatti Type 370. In the former, the hands are turned by engine-inspired drive belts rather than traditional gears. The latter has a movement built between five plates arranged along a horizontal axis in a shape resembling a car engine.

What company has a watch called the "Roadster"?
Cartier. It is a sports watch with tonneau-shaped case, introduced in 2002.

In 2003, Breitling brought out a watch named after which car company?
Bentley. The watch is a chronograph bearing the label "Breitling for Bentley," and its design was inspired by the Bentley Continental GT, introduced in 2003. The watch bezel, which has a cross-hashed pattern, resembles the car's dashboard and radiator grille. The watch's crown is knurled like the buttons on the car's dashboard. Breitling has brought out other "Breitling for Bentley" watches since the 2003 original.

After what Formula 1 driver did Audemars Piguet name a Royal Oak model launched in 2004?
Juan Pablo Montoya. The watch was called the Royal Oak Offshore Juan Pablo Montoya Chronograph. It had several race-car-inspired details, such as the cooling-flap shape of the chronograph buttons and a crown shaped like a wheel axle.

What grandson of a car-company founder launched a line of watches now manufactured by Eterna?
F.A. Porsche, grandson of Ferdinand Porsche, founder of the famous Porsche car company of Germany. F.A. Porsche's company is called Porsche Design, and markets a variety of sleekly styled consumer products. Porsche Design bought the Swiss watch company Eterna SA in 1995, and the latter now manufactures Porsche Design watches.

What were "motorities"?
A collection of often-oddball driving accessories and instruments, including timepieces, marketed by the

British company Alfred Dunhill in the early 1900s.
The timepieces included a stopwatch called the
"speedograph" that drivers could use in conjunction
with road milestones to measure their speed, and a
watch that could be fit on the steering wheel of a car.
Non-timepiece items included an "umbrella coat,"
which protected the driver of an open car from the
rain, and a pair of strap-on binoculars called "Bobby
Finders," which enabled drivers to spot policemen in
time to slow down to a legal speed (in those days, 12
mph or less). The modern Dunhill company, A.
Dunhill, markets a watch whose two prominent
subdials were inspired by the Bobby Finders.

What was the Auto-Graph?
A chronograph wristwatch introduced by Heuer (now
TAG Heuer) in 1948. It had a chronograph with
tachymeter scale and a special feature for determining
fuel consumption, which consisted of a push-button
that moved the center hand in increments around
the dial.

WATCHES AND ROYALTY

Royal favorite Robert Dudley, Earl of Leicester, gave to Queen Elizabeth I a watch believed by some historians to have been a notable "first." What "first" was it?

The first watch worn on the wrist. The watch is described in a document of the time as an "armlet or shakell of golde, all fairely garnishedd with rubyes and dyamondes, haveing in the closeing thearof a clocke." The watch itself no longer exists.

What watch company named a watch after Queen Elizabeth I?

Bulova. In the mid-20th century it named a wrist-watch "Elizabeth" in honor of the queen, who is said by some to have been the world's first wristwatch owner.

During her coronation in 1953, Queen Elizabeth II of England wore a very unusual watch. What made it noteworthy?

It was the world's smallest watch. The movement, a joint effort by the Jaeger and LeCoultre companies in 1929 (they were to merge officially in 1937) was just under 5 millimeters across. Cartier, which cased the movement, presented her with the watch in 1938. To this day the 101 remains the smallest mechanical movement ever made.

In 1872 Queen Victoria gave her equerry and friend John Brown a watch in thanks for a favor. What was the favor?
His rescuing her from a pistol-wielding student who attacked her in front of Buckingham Palace. The watch bore the inscription: "To my faithful and devoted personal attendant John Brown Esquire in grateful remembrance of the presence of mind and courage he displayed at Buckingham Palace Feb. 29 1872, from Victoria R."

In 1851, Queen Victoria visited the famous Great Exhibition at London's Crystal Palace and bought herself a watch made by a young watch firm whose reputation and prospects the sale greatly enhanced. What company was it?
Patek Philippe. The piece was a keyless-winding, baby-blue enamel pendant watch (the color was said to match Victoria's eyes) adorned with diamonds. Victoria also bought a Patek for her beloved husband Prince Albert. Victoria's patronage gave the company, then just 12 years old, a major boost and set a trend among other royalty.

A Mickey Mouse watch once caused disruption in a certain royal household. Whose household was it?
That of Japan's Emperor Hirohito. One day in 1978, Hirohito was disconcerted to find that his beloved Mickey Mouse watch, which had been given to him after a tour of Disneyland 3 years earlier and had seldom left his wrist since, had stopped running. His

aides were unable to diagnose the problem. Finally, a watch expert told them the watch needed a new battery.

Which royals visited the factory of the Tissot watch company in Le Locle in 1960?
Princess Grace and Prince Rainier of Monaco. During the visit, between 2,000 and 2,500 people waited outside the factory for a glimpse of the couple, who stayed for 45 minutes. The princess, a local paper reported, wore no watch. When the visit ended, Tissot chief Édouard-Louis Tissot gave the princess gifts of a watch and music box for the royal children Caroline and Albert.

One of Prince Charles's watches was stolen during a 1994 break-in at St. James Palace in London. What watch was it?
A Movado that had been a gift from Charles's god-mother, Lady Braubourne, daughter of Earl Mount-batten. The watch was a sports model with black crocodile cover and was engraved "Charles from his Godmother Patricia."

What company markets a "Prince Charles" watch?
Chopard. The watch, a tonneau, was the result of a conversation the prince had in 1999 with Caroline Gruosi-Scheufele, whose family owns the Chopard watch and jewelry company. The conversation took place during a dinner at Highgrove House, the prince's residence. Gruosi-Scheufele told the prince about the limited-edition watches that Chopard makes for the Carreras Foundation, a charity headed by Jose Carreras. Charles then asked Chopard to make a special watch for his charity, the Prince's Foundation. Chopard did, launching first a men's mechanical model, with a twin-barreled LUC 4.96

movement, and then a women's quartz version. Part of the proceeds from sales of the watch go to the prince's charity.

Abraham-Louis Breguet made for one member of royalty a very early wristwatch, said by some to be the first watch with a case specifically designed to be worn on the wrist. For whom did Breguet make it?
Caroline Murat, the queen of Naples, who was installed on the throne by her brother, Napoleon Bonaparte. The watch, purchased in 1811, had an oblong case and a wristband made of hair intertwined with gold thread. Some argue that this timepiece was the first true wristwatch because it was specifically designed to be worn on the wrist, whereas earlier wrist-worn watches were merely watch pendants affixed to bracelets. The watch was just one of dozens that Caroline Murat bought from Breguet; she was his best customer.

King Constantine of Greece helped boost the popularity of what watch brand among other members of royalty?
Hublot. In the early 1980s, he bought a Hublot watch for himself and gave one to his brother-in-law, King Carlos of Spain. King Gustav of Sweden then also began wearing a Hublot, as did Prince Albert and Princesses Caroline and Stephanie of Monaco, Queen Noor of Jordan and others.

What British king was an ardent amateur horologist whose personal effects included his notes on the right way to take apart a watch?
George III. He not only tinkered with watches, but also built himself a royal observatory at Kew where he tested one of John Harrison's chronometers. In

addition, he was an invaluable patron of such watch-makers as Thomas Mudge and John Arnold.

What 20th-century ousted king owned a watch collection deemed to be among the most important in the world?

King Farouk of Egypt, who was overthrown in a military coup in 1952. The Egyptian government confiscated his watch collection, which included not only technological masterpieces but also an amazing array of erotic watches. Sotheby's auctioned off the watches in March 1954.

The "royal" in the name of Audemars Piguet's best-known watch, the Royal Oak, refers to what member of royalty?

Charles II of England. According to a famous legend in British history, Charles in 1651 sought refuge from Oliver Cromwell's troops in the hollow of an oak tree, which came to be known as the Royal Oak. In the 18th century, the British navy began naming ships after the Royal Oak. The bezel of the Royal Oak watch is shaped like a porthole in homage to those ships.

What imprisoned member of royalty ordered a watch from Abraham-Louis Breguet?

Marie Antoinette. She ordered the watch in 1792 while in the Temple prison (she was guillotined the next year). The queen had been a Breguet customer since 1782, when she bought from him a perpetuelle (i.e., self-winding) repeater with calendar, and her patronage helped launch him on the path to become the most famous watchmaker of his time.

King James II of England was the arbiter in a bitter horological dispute. What was it about?

Who should receive the patent for the repeating watch. The contenders were the famous watchmaker Daniel Quare and the inventor and clergyman Edward Barlow, who was working in conjunction with the celebrated horologist Thomas Tompion. In 1687, James heard the arguments on both sides, tried out both watches, and awarded the patent to Quare.

What is the so-called "Queen's Watch"?
A watch made by the great British watchmaker Thomas Mudge for Queen Charlotte, wife of King George III, in 1770. It was the first watch to contain a lever escapement, standard equipment in mechanical watches today, and for that reason is among the most famous watches in the world.

What king picked Winston Churchill's watch from his pocket?
King Farouk of Egypt. In 1942, Churchill went to Egypt to visit the British troops fighting the Germans there. He stopped in Cairo and had dinner with Farouk at the Mena House Hotel. The king was a kleptomaniac (in some circles he was called "The Thief of Cairo") and, thanks to lessons he had taken from a master thief, an expert pickpocket. He was also an inveterate practical joker. During dinner he lifted Churchill's pocket watch. When Churchill discovered his loss minutes later, Farouk excused himself, supposedly to try to apprehend the thief. He soon returned with Churchill's watch, blaming the theft on a palace employee.

What prince once owned a chain of watch stores?
Prince Jefri Bolkiah, younger brother of the sultan of Brunei. The chain, called Watches of Switzerland, was owned by Asprey & Garrard, which in turn was owned by Prince Jefri. Asprey sold the chain in 1998.

Prince Jefri surrendered Asprey & Garrard in 2000 as part of an out-of-court settlement with the Brunei Investment Agency, an arm of the Brunei government, from which the prince was accused of embezzling billions of dollars.

FOUNDING FATHERS

The putative founder of the watchmaking industry in Switzerland's Jura Mountain region is honored with a statue in the town of Le Locle. Who is he?
Daniel JeanRichard. Born in the village of La Sagne, near Le Locle, in 1665, he set up a watchmaking workshop that engendered many others in the area. Although he is sometimes described as the father of Jura watchmaking, historians now believe he was just one of its early practitioners. JeanRichard used a manufacturing method called *établissage*, in which he depended on specialized outside suppliers to make parts and perform various manufacturing operations. This division of labor, which became a hallmark of the Jura, was key to the region's watchmaking success.

Who founded a watch company to help alleviate the abysmal poverty of a region in what is now Germany?
Ferdinand Adolph Lange. A highly skilled watch-maker, Lange received a loan from the kingdom of Saxony to set up a watchmaking school and factory in the small town of Glashütte, just south of Dresden. The town and surrounding area desperately needed a

new industry; its inhabitants earned their living mostly from crafts and hardscrabble farming. Lange's company was founded in 1845 and called A. Lange & Söhne. (After German reunification, in 1990, the company was re-established in Glashütte.) It gave rise to many other watch firms as his former employees set up businesses of their own. In the following decades, Glashütte became an internationally famous watchmaking center.

Rolex founder Hans Wilsdorf bore on his body a sure sign of his life in the watch business. What was it?
A permanent callus on his right thumb caused by constantly winding and setting watches.

After founding, in 1946, what later became Casio Computer Co., Tadao Kashio scored his first big success with what product?
A finger ring called the "yubiwa pipe" that could hold a cigarette, thus allowing the smoker to keep his hands free. It also enabled him to smoke his cigarette down to the very end, a selling point in postwar Japan, where consumer products were scarce. Kashio produced the rings for two years, turning out 200 to 300 per day. He used the profits to finance research on calculators, which became Casio's specialty after the company perfected a totally electronic model (weighing 120 kilos) in 1957. In 1974, Casio introduced its first watch, a digital model called the Casiotron, which was equipped with a perpetual calendar and told the time in multiple time zones.

Achille Ditesheim started a watch company when he was just 19 years old. What company was it?
The company now called Movado (it was so named in 1905). He founded the firm in 1881 in La Chaux-de-

Fonds, hiring six craftsmen and setting up a small factory at 13, rue 1er Mars.

In 1868 an American watchmaker moved to Switzerland to found what watch company?
International Watch Company (IWC) Schaffhausen. Because the Civil War had greatly reduced the labor supply in America, IWC's founder, a Boston watchmaker named Florentine Ariosto Jones, chose Switzerland as the site of his new company.

What watch company was founded by a count?
Patek Philippe. The Polish Count Antoine Norbert de Patek founded the company in 1839 with countryman François Czapek. The partnership was later dissolved and the French watchmaker Adrien Philippe became Patek's partner in 1845.

What watch brand founder, known as the "Master of Complications," left his company in 2003 due to disagreements with his partner?
Franck Muller. In 2004, he and his partner, Vartan Sirmakes, were reconciled and Muller returned to the company (based in Genthod, near Geneva) as a consultant.

Jaeger-LeCoultre founder Charles-Antoine LeCoultre, inventor of many watchmaking tools, is best known for which one?
The millionometer, which made it possible for watchmakers to measure microns (millionths of a meter) for the first time. LeCoultre made his first millionometer in 1844. It helped spur acceptance of the metric system by the watch industry.

What livestock-related device did Édouard Heuer, founder of what is today TAG Heuer, invent?

A cattle counter. Designed in 1890, it enabled farmers to keep track of their herds.

In 1887, at age 47, Édouard Heuer, founder of what is today TAG Heuer, abruptly handed over control of the company to his son, Jules-Édouard, forever. Why?
He was profoundly depressed by the death of his daughter, Louise, who died of burns from a fire caused by a freak cooking accident.

What watch company founder started out as a ticket scalper?
Tom Kartsotis, chairman of Fossil, Inc. He founded the company in 1984 with his future wife, Lynne Stafford, along with Mike Barnes and Alan Moore. They used money they had made scalping tickets in Texas, where the practice is legal.

What watch company founder is the most powerful person in the watch industry?
Nicolas G. Hayek, founder of SMH (now called the Swatch Group). Hayek formed the company in 1983 by engineering the merger of Switzerland's two troubled watchmaking conglomerates, ASUAG and SSIH. The Swatch Group now owns or licenses 17 watch brands and makes movements through its ETA, Manufacture Breguet (formerly Nouvelle Lemania) and Frédéric Piguet subsidiaries. (ETA also makes finished Swatch watches.) In addition, the company produces a huge range of watch components under such names as Nivarox (oscillators, escapements, balance springs), Universo (watch hands) and Renata (watch batteries). In 2004, the Swatch Group had sales of just over 4 billion Swiss francs (more than 3 billion of them were from finished watches). Hayek is Swatch Group chairman.

What watch company founder, while on a trip to America, wrote irritably to his co-workers in Switzerland: "…The Americans demand above all inexpensive watches which, nevertheless, should allow them to determine the speed of their horses to an accuracy of ¼ of a second"?

Antoine Norbert de Patek, co-founder of Patek Philippe. Patek made many foreign trips to sell his company's watches, including one to America in 1854-55 that lasted many months. It brought him much woe: his hotel room was robbed, one boat he was on caught fire, a second one ran aground for three days and then collided with another boat, and a snowstorm stranded him for four days on the prairie.

What future watch-company founder was arrested by Castro's government and spent 8 hours in a Cuban jail expecting to be killed?

Movado Group founder and chairman Gedalio "Gerry" Grinberg. Soon after Castro's revolution, the Cuban-born Grinberg, who was then the distributor in Cuba for Omega and Piaget, was seized by the secret police and accused of being a counter-revolutionary and of working for the CIA. Neither charge was true, and Grinberg thinks the arrest may have been due to his having turned down a job with the revolutionary government. The police told him he would be executed and subjected him to 8 hours of threats and verbal abuse. They then released him without explanation. Within a few days he, his wife and their children fled Cuba for the United States. He founded North American Watch Corp., now called the Movado Group, in 1965.

The founder of Robert Ingersoll and Bro., a forerunner of today's Timex Corp., was involved in a lurid and highly publicized scandal concerning

his personal life. What caused the scandal?
His estranged wife's attempt to murder her lover, followed by her suicide. In 1926, Robert Ingersoll's wife shot and seriously wounded her 60-year-old paramour when he announced he was abandoning her and returning to his wife. The 55-year-old Mrs. Ingersoll then killed herself. The event was reported on the front page of the *New York Times*. According to another newspaper, Mrs. Ingersoll was wearing a pink negligee and $35,000 worth of jewelry when she died. The *Times* described her husband, who had made a fortune from his company's famous Dollar Watch, as "the most pathetic figure of them all," frail, stooped, and walking with canes. He died two years later at age 69.

The founder of the once-prolific watch industry in Besançon, France, died a disgraced pauper after a series of humiliating events. Who was he?
Laurent Mégevand. In Geneva, at the start of his watchmaking career, the Swiss-born Mégevand was twice accused of underkarating, i.e., selling gold that was less pure than he claimed it to be. He fled first to Le Locle, Switzerland, and then to Besançon, where in 1793 he set up a watch factory, the first one in that city. He was accused of embezzling from the factory and forced to resign. He spent the last years of his life writing sycophantic poems about Napoleon, hoping to win government support. It never came, and he died a pauper in 1814. The company he founded, the Fabrique National de Besançon, nonetheless became the cornerstone of a watch industry that would thrive throughout the 19th century. The region around Besançon is still home to many watch companies, which make both finished watches and components, the latter chiefly for watch manufacturers across the nearby Swiss border.

GAME TIME

**Which watch company was the first official timer
of the Olympic Games?**
Heuer, predecessor of today's TAG Heuer. It debuted
as official timer at the 1920 summer games in
Antwerp. From 1896 until then, judges had used
chronographs made by several different companies.
Heuer, which specialized in chronographs, also timed
the summer Olympics in 1924 and '28.

**Which watch company timed the famed 1936
Olympics, where, to the chagrin of Adolf Hitler,
the African-American Jesse Owens won four gold
medals for track-and-field events?**
Omega. The company's stopwatches timed Owens's
victories in the 100-meter, 200-meter and 4 x 100-
meter relay (Owens also won a gold medal in the long
jump). All told, Omega has timed 20 Olympic
competitions, more than any other watch brand. In
four of these Olympics, those in 1976, '80, '84 and
'88, Omega joined with Longines in a joint venture
called Swiss Timing. Omega will again time the
Olympics in 2006, '08 and '10 in Turin, Beijing and
Vancouver, respectively.

When was quartz technology first used to time the Olympics?
In 1952, for the summer games in Helsinki, Finland. That year, Omega introduced its quartz-based Time Recorder, which timed and printed results to 1/100 of a second.

In the 1992 summer games in Barcelona, Olympic timer Seiko determined that Gail Devers had won the 100-meter dash in one of the most astonishingly close finishes in Olympic history, one that looked to the naked eye like a five-way tie. How much time separated Devers from the fifth-place runner?
A minuscule 6/100 of a second. Seiko's Slit-Video 1000 system, which photographed the runners at the instant they crossed the finish line, told viewers what their own eyes could not, that Devers had won by 2/100 of a second.

In 1982, a commercial that aired during the Super Bowl featured the president of a major watch brand. He wasn't touting his watch, though, but something entirely different. Who was he and what was he promoting?
Hugh Glenn, then president of Omega's U.S. subsidiary, appeared on behalf of United Airlines.

What is a "yacht timer"?
A watch feature that counts down the 10 minutes before the start of a yacht race. The pre-race minutes are crucial to the race's competitors, who use that time to gain speed and maneuver their boats up to the starting line so they'll be in good position when the starting signal sounds. A yacht timer marks the passage of each remaining minute. Some yacht timers also mark the passing seconds.

The famous Jaeger-LeCoultre Reverso, whose case can be flipped over so it is upside down, was designed for participants in what sport?

Polo. The Reverso, introduced in 1931, came into being when British army officers based in India asked a representative of the LeCoultre watch company for a wristwatch whose crystal would remain intact even when subjected to the jarring blows of a polo match. LeCoultre consulted with the Jaeger watch firm (Jaeger and LeCoultre merged in 1937), which enlisted the help of designer and engineer René-Alfred Chauvot. He designed a watch whose case could be turned over to protect the crystal.

What is the defining feature of a sports watch?

Enough water resistance so the watch can be worn swimming (i.e., it must have a water-resistance level of at least 50 meters). Of course, many sports watches have additional features such as luminous hands, a rotating bezel and/or a chronograph function.

What watch brands has golf great Tiger Woods endorsed?

First, beginning in 1997, Rolex's Tudor brand, and then, starting in 2003, TAG Heuer. In 2005, TAG Heuer introduced the Tiger Woods Professional Golf Watch, a square, lightweight watch with a crown at 9 o'clock instead of 3 o'clock to prevent its digging into a golfer's bent wrist.

The Timex Ironman, introduced in 1984, was named for the annual Ironman competition. What is it?

A triathlon consisting of a 2.4-mile swim, 112-mile bike ride and 26.2-mile run. The world championship is held annually in Kalua-Kona, Hawaii. There are many Ironman qualifying races around the world.

The first Ironman Triathlon took place in 1978.

In 2002, Piaget enlisted as spokesman for its new Upstream watch a former Olympic athlete with an unorthodox approach to his sport. Who was he and why did Piaget choose him?
The athlete was Dick Fosbury, a high-jumper on the 1968 U.S. Olympic team. Unable to master the conventional, arm-first, face-down high-jumping method, Fosbury perfected his own system, throwing himself head-first, face-up over the bar. The maneuver became known as the "Fosbury Flop." Piaget thought Fosbury would be the perfect representative for the Upstream: the watch was put on and taken off by means of its bezel, which folded in on itself and locked into position face-up in a Fosbury Flop-like manner.

In 1979 Piaget introduced a watch named after a particular sport. What sport was it?
Polo. The Piaget Polo became the brand's best-known model.

What watch model is named after a famous horseracing venue?
The Saratoga, a high-end sports watch in the Concord brand. It was named after the Saratoga racetrack in upstate New York.

In 1998 a watch-company-sponsored team played the central role in a major sports scandal. What was the scandal?
Team Festina, sponsored by the Festina watch brand, was expelled from the Tour de France for using performance-enhancing drugs. Police then began investigating drug use by other teams, leading to several protests and the withdrawal of many riders

from the competition. By the end of the Tour, six of the original 14 teams had dropped out. The French press dubbed the troubles "l'affaire Festina." Festina dropped sponsorship of the team but became the official timer of the race.

In the 1990s a famous baseball player gave a teammate a $16,000 Rolex as thanks for a favor. Who was the player and what was the favor?

The player was Roger Clemens. After he joined the Toronto Blue Jays in 1997, he gave the Rolex to his new teammate, Carlos Delgado, as thanks for (or, at least one sports columnist suggested, in return for) Delgado's giving up his number, 21, so that Clemens could have it. Clemens had played under that number for the Boston Red Sox and believed it brought him good luck.

In the early 1950s, U.S. Time (now Timex) marketed a watch bearing the signature of a famous golfer. Who was it?

Ben Hogan. The watch sold for $14.95, nearly twice the price of some other Timex celebrity-endorsed or character watches of the time.

What famous ex-athlete was on the board of directors of the company that marketed Swiss Army brand watches?

O. J. Simpson. At the time of his ex-wife's murder he was on the board of directors of the Forschner Group, which owned the Swiss Army brand of watches. His board membership was seen by some as a macabre coincidence because, despite its strong watch business, Forschner was best known for its knives (Swiss Army pocketknives and Sabatier cutlery). Simpson's connection to the company was spotlighted in a deposition from a limousine driver who drove

Simpson from a Forschner board meeting just three days before the murders of Nicole Brown Simpson and Ronald Goldman. The driver said that Simpson, in the back seat, had pulled out a knife (knives had been offered as gifts to board members at the meeting) and demonstrated how it could be used to kill someone. In his own deposition, Simpson denied the incident had taken place.

What watch is known as the "Jean Claude Killy" watch, after the skier who won three gold medals at the Olympics in 1968?
The Rolex reference 6036, a manual-wind chronograph with triple date. The watch got its nickname because it was Killy's favorite Rolex of the 25 he owned.

In October 1981 in New York, Ernst Thomke, then head of the movement maker ETA and soon to be one of the heroes of the Swiss-watch-industry revival, performed an impressive athletic feat. What was it?
He ran the New York marathon with a broken foot in 3 hours, 57 minutes. Thomke ran the race to win a bet with Gedalio "Gerry" Grinberg, head of North American Watch Corp. (now the Movado Group), who challenged Thomke's assertion that running 26 miles was not particularly difficult, and offered him $1,000 if he could finish the race in under 4 hours. Thomke, then in his early 40s, and never having run a marathon, flew from Switzerland to New York especially for the race. Six miles into it, he tripped and broke a bone in his right foot. Undeterred, he ran on, crossing the finish line within the allotted time, his right foot swollen to jumbo size.

What prominent watch company executive was

once a member of the Swiss Olympic ski team?
Philippe Stern, owner of Patek Philippe. He was
on the team while a university student but gave up
competitive skiing when he was injured in an accident.

**In 1992, Laurence Grunstein, president of Citizen
Watch Co. of America, became the world's first
"17th man." What does that mean?**
In the America's Cup competition, teams, which have
16 members, are, according to a rule passed in 1992,
allowed to take on their boats one non-team-member,
i.e., a "17th man." Grunstein became the first such
passenger, at the invitation of yachting legend Dennis
Conner. He sailed aboard Team Dennis Conner's
boat, the Stars & Stripes, in the first race of the
Defender Series, which determined who would
defend the Cup against the challenger. Conner
invited him because Citizen had recently signed on as
sponsor of Team Dennis Conner. (Citizen was also
the official timer of the Defender Series, the Challenger Series, and the America's Cup races.) Stars &
Stripes lost the race to Bill Koch's America3, which
went on to win the Cup.

WATCHES AND WATER

What is "H-4"?

It stands for "Harrison 4" and is the name of the fourth timepiece that John Harrison produced in his lifelong effort to make a timepiece that could be used to determine the longitude at sea. H-4, completed in 1759, was astoundingly precise: during an 81-day test voyage from Britain to Jamaica, it lost a mere 5 seconds. Rupert Gould, a timepiece historian who spent 17 years restoring Harrison's marine clocks, called H-4 "the most famous timekeeper which ever has been or ever will be made." Harrison's timepieces are now exhibited in the National Maritime Museum in Greenwich, England.

In the days before radar and other modern navigation techniques, marine chronometers were used to determine longitude. How?

Sailors used them to keep track of the time at a point of known longitude, such as the Greenwich meridian, so they could figure their distance east or west of that point, i.e., their longitude. To calculate that distance, they needed to determine, by celestial observation, the time at their present location. They then compared that time with the time indicated on the marine chronometer, which had been set precisely to Greenwich mean time (or whatever reference time they had chosen) at the start of the voyage. They could then translate that time difference into degrees of longitude.

What event caused Britain to establish the Longitude Act, which led to the development of the marine chronometer?
The wreck in 1707 of four British warships on the Scilly Isles, off the coast of England. The wreck claimed 2,000 lives. The ships crashed into the islands because the sailors did not know their longitude. Seven years later the Longitude Act was passed, providing for a prize of 20,000 pounds sterling (equivalent to about $5 million today) to be given to anyone who could devise an effective method of determining longitude. The marine chronometer provided that method.

Even though he was the first to develop an accurate marine clock, John Harrison is not considered to be the father of the marine chronometer. Who is?
Pierre Le Roy. In 1766, Le Roy completed a marine clock with a so-called "detached" escapement, which, unlike the escapement in Harrison's clock, prevented friction from interfering with the oscillations of the balance. Le Roy's clock had two other novel features: a new type of compensation balance and an isochronized balance spring. Although subsequent marine chronometers were quite different from Le Roy's, he is credited with paving the way for them with these innovations.

In the 1930s, Longines introduced a watch that could help fog-bound ships find their way. How did the watch do that?

The watch, called the Nautical Stop-second, had a chronograph and telemeter scale, which were used in conjunction with signals sent by the U.S. Lighthouse Service via its distance-finding stations. When there was fog, the stations emitted simultaneous radio and sound signals every three minutes. By timing the interval between receiving the radio signal and hearing the sound, navigators could, using the watch's telemeter scale, determine the ship's distance from the station.

How did Eterna's Kon Tiki watch get its name?
The watch was named for the balsawood raft piloted by Thor Heyerdahl and his five-man crew (all wearing Eterna watches) on their famous 1947 voyage from Peru to Polynesia. The purpose of the grueling, 97-day trip was to prove that prehistoric people could have crossed the Pacific Ocean on primitive craft like the Kon Tiki. Eterna introduced its Kon Tiki collection of watches in 1958.

In 1997, a Breitling watch helped save the lives of a crew on an ocean expedition. What were the circumstances?
The crew was that of the Mata-Rangi, a reed raft designed to resemble vessels supposedly used by Easter Islanders thousands of years ago. The watch that saved them was the Breitling Emergency, which is equipped with a transmitter that can, by means of a pull-out antenna, broadcast a distress signal to rescuers. In an effort to re-create the migration of prehistoric peoples, the Mata-Rangi, whose sponsors included Breitling, had set out on a Pacific voyage of thousands of miles when it encountered a storm and started to break up 1,800 nautical miles from the Chilean coast. Kitin Munoz, the Spanish explorer who headed the mission, activated his Emergency

watch, sending a signal picked up by a commercial aircraft, which found the craft and relayed its position to the Chilean authorities. An American yacht named the Stray Dog headed for the Mata-Rangi and rescued the crew of 13.

Who was Mercedes Gleitze?
The first Englishwoman to swim the English Channel, and, for that reason, the centerpiece of a promotional campaign by Rolex for its water-resistant Oyster watch. Gleitze swam the channel on Oct. 7, 1927, on her eighth attempt. Because questions were raised about the validity of her performance, Gleitze announced she would repeat the swim on Oct. 21. Rolex founder Hans Wilsdorf, upon hearing of the planned ninth swim, asked her to carry with her a Rolex Oyster to prove its impermeability to water. She did so, and signed a letter of endorsement for the watch afterward. She did not make it across the channel on this attempt. Rolex nonetheless used Gleitze's picture and references to her prior swim to promote the Oyster.

What is the purpose of the helium escape valves found on some dive watches?
They release the helium that has built up inside the watch case and thus prevent the watch crystal from popping off because of gas pressure. Such a valve is of use only on very deep dives requiring a pressurized chamber in which the diver breathes, instead of normal air, a special gas mixture containing helium. In such instances, the helium in the chamber permeates the watch case and, if the gas is not released, can cause the crystal to blow off like a Champagne cork.

Cartier's modern-day Pasha watch was named after a water-resistant watch from the 1930s. How did

the original Pasha watch come into being?

It was made for the Pasha of Marrakesh, who had asked Cartier to make him a watch he could wear in the swimming pool. It is not known what the original Pasha looked like, but one writer suggests it was a water-resistant Tank model. Today's Pasha was modeled on a Cartier design from the 1940s.

In 2001, Audemars Piguet sponsored a racing yacht that scored a major "first." What first was it?

It was the first European competitor to win the America's Cup. The yacht hailed from Switzerland and was called the Alinghi. Audemars Piguet named a version of its Royal Oak watch after it.

What was the Fast 2000-Be Happy?

A boat sponsored in 1999 by Audemars Piguet in the America's Cup competition. It was the first America's Cup competitor from Switzerland. Despite the boat's name, its fate was anything but happy. Its mast broke and the team withdrew from the competition, pulling out of the Louis Vuitton Cup Challenger Series, which determines who will challenge the winner of the Defender Series in the America's Cup races.

One of Corum's best-known watches has a marine-related name. What is it?

The Admiral's Cup. It was named for a series of races held every other year at Cowes, England, off the Isle of Wight. The watch's best-known feature is the band of 12 maritime flags around the bezel or dial, which represent the numbers 1 through 12 in the maritime code. The first version of the watch, which had a square case, was introduced in 1960, 3 years after the first Admiral's Cup competition. In 1982, the watch was redesigned with the 12-sided case it has today.

A Rolex watch participated in a world-record-breaking sea-related event in 1953. What event was it?

Auguste and Jacques Piccard's 3,150-meter descent into the Tyrrhenian Sea in a submersible called the Trieste. It was the deepest dive anyone had ever made. To prove the extreme impermeability of one of its new watch models, Rolex affixed it to the craft's exterior. The watch survived unharmed. Afterward, Rolex put the watch into production (the series-manufactured version was water-resistant to 200 meters), naming it the Submariner.

Rolex's Sea Dweller, introduced in 1971, was based on the Submariner but had a special added device. What was it?

A helium escape valve. The valve was added because the watch was to be used on very deep dives (it was developed specifically for divers working to tap offshore oil reserves).

In 1997, the luxury conglomerate Vendôme (now the Richemont Group) bought a brand of divers' watches that have since become very fashionable. What brand was it?

Panerai. The brand, now headquartered in Milan, had been a supplier of watches and other instruments to the Italian Navy before and during World War II.

How many watches did diving-watch specialist Panerai make between the company's birth in the 19th century and the Panerai brand's re-introduction in 1993?

About 300. The company spent its first decades making military instruments and only began manufacturing watches in 1938. For many years after that, virtually its only watch customers were the Italian and

Egyptian navies, which placed very small orders.

What watch company makes a model called the Overseas?
Vacheron Constantin. It launched the watch, a rugged sports model, in 1996.

Why do the rotating bezels on divers' watches turn in only one direction?
For safety reasons. They turn counterclockwise only, so that if the watch is accidentally knocked during a dive, the bezel will not be pushed clockwise. If it were, the elapsed time indicated on the bezel would be less than the actual elapsed time. That would be dangerous to a diver using the bezel to time his or her dive.

TIME AND THE ARTS

The earliest known painting showing a watch dates from when?
Circa 1558. The painting, by Tommaso Manzuoli, shows a man holding up a German-made watch that has an hour hand only. By his side, on a table, sits a detachable alarm mechanism and its carrying case. The work belongs to the Science Museum in London.

One of Salvador Dali's most famous paintings, finished in 1931, is a landscape containing limp watches, one of them hanging from a tree. What is the painting's name?
The Persistence of Memory. The painting depicts three pocket watches that appear to have melted. A fourth, unmelted one, is covered with ants. Dali referred to the watches, whose softness is like that of over-ripe cheese, as "the camembert of space and time" and wrote in his autobiography that he was inspired to paint them after eating some camembert cheese for dinner. He revisited the soft-watch theme in *The Disintegration of the Persistence of Memory,* completed in 1954. In it, the watches appear to be falling apart and are under water.

Who painted *The Theft of a Watch*?
The British social satirist and moralist William
Hogarth. The picture, dating from 1731, depicts a
group of prostitutes in a brothel surreptitiously
stealing a customer's watch.

**In what famous operetta is a watch used as proof of
a husband's infidelity?**
Die Fledermaus, by Johann Strauss, Jr. In that work,
the lead male character, Gabriel von Eisenstein,
attends a masquerade ball where he flirts extrava-
gantly with a woman who is disguised as a Hungarian
countess but who, unbeknownst to him, is actually
his wife, Rosalinda. In a piece entitled "The Watch
Duet," the "countess" persuades von Eisenstein to give
her his watch so she will have proof of his deception.
Later, when he expresses indignation to Rosalinda at
an extramarital flirtation of her own, she counters his
attack by showing him the watch he gave her in her
countess disguise.

**What watch company produced an Artists Series of
watches with models designed by Andy Warhol,
Yaacov Agam, Arman, James Rosenquist, Max Bill
and Romero Britto?**
Movado. It introduced the watches, one at a time,
between 1988 and 1994. All were produced in small
series; a total of just 2,479 pieces were made.

**What famous artist made several detailed references
in his diary to parties he attended that were given
by Movado Group founder Gedalio Grinberg?**
Andy Warhol, who kept a day-by-day record of his
social life that was published after his death in 1987
under the title *The Andy Warhol Diaries*. Grinberg, an
art enthusiast, invited Warhol to several Movado
Group lunches and dinners in New York (the com-

pany was then called North American Watch Corp.) in the late 1970s and early '80s. At one, Warhol sat next to a woman who seemed to think he was Truman Capote. At another, he writes, "Mr. Grinberg pushed me into General Haig and he was sweet, we talked about his interview in *Interview*." At yet another, he enjoyed a "good" lunch of steak and potatoes while listening to Gerald Ford give a speech. When Warhol had spoken briefly with Ford earlier at the luncheon, the ex-president had seemed a little distracted or confused, Warhol writes, but at the podium he appeared to be more focused. "Once he got started on his speech he didn't seem so out of it at all, he remembered the whole speech," Warhol writes.

Franz Joseph Haydn wrote a piece of music with a horological nickname. What piece was it?
The Clock Symphony, number 101, written in 1794. The symphony became known by this name because the main melody in its second movement is played against an accompaniment that sounds like a clock ticking.

In 1996, Sotheby's auctioned off an oil painting entitled *The Watchmaker* for nearly $1 million, setting what was then a record for works by this man. Who is it?
Norman Rockwell. The painting showed a wizened old watchmaker working at his bench as a young boy looked on in fascination.

What celebrated architect was born in the famous Swiss watchmaking town of La Chaux-de-Fonds and was the son of a watch-dial enameller?
Le Corbusier (né Charles-Édouard Jeanneret-Gris), one of the main proponents of the International Style. He lived in La Chaux-de-Fonds until he was

29. As a teenager, he studied watch-case engraving at the local trade school, but was advised by a teacher that he should become an architect, a path he followed after studying painting.

What watch company owns a landmark building designed in 1916 by the renowned architect Le Corbusier?

The Movado Group. It acquired the building, which is in La Chaux-de-Fonds, Switzerland, in 2004 as part of its purchase of the Ebel watch brand. The building is called "la Villa Turque" because it was inspired by the Byzantine architecture that Le Corbusier had seen during a trip to the Bosporus in what is now Turkey. It was built for the watch industry magnate Anatole Schwob, whose factory made watches for the Cyma and Tavannes brands.

For several years, Vacheron Constantin ran a print advertising campaign featuring a certain painting. What did it depict?

A watchmaking workshop in 18th-century Geneva. The picture was meant to evoke Vacheron's long history in that city. It was painted by the Victorian artist Christophe François de Ziegler (1855-1909) and is on display in Geneva's Museum of Art and History.

Who designed Rado's Carpe Diem watch, which was introduced in 2002?

Karl Gerstner, a Swiss artist and graphic designer. The watch's dial is decorated with arcs composed of colors that change with the passing seconds while a white dot and wedge-shaped pointer mark the hours and minutes. The name is Latin for "seize the day."

The artists Kiki Picasso, Keith Haring and Mimmo

Paladino all designed watches for which watch brand?

Swatch. The watches were all part of the brand's "Art Special" series, inaugurated in 1985.

In 1996, Jaeger-LeCoultre introduced a series of Reverso watches decorated with enameled reproductions of lithographs by whom?

The Czech artist Alfonse Mucha, a famous proponent of the Art Nouveau style who is best known for his posters of Sarah Bernhardt. There were four watches, each enameled on its case back with one of Mucha's turn-of-the-century *Four Seasons* lithographs, in which four young women represent the seasons.

WHERE OH WHERE?

What city was once believed to be the birthplace of the watch?
Nuremberg, Germany. That's where Peter Henlein, often described as the father of the watch, plied his trade. Henlein was a very talented locksmith, and later watchmaker, who made watches in the early 1500s, earlier than any other known artisan. Nonetheless, experts now agree it is unlikely he made the very first watch, which was probably the work of someone whose name has not survived.

What area in Switzerland's Jura Mountains is famous for the complicated movements made there?
The Vallée de Joux (Joux Valley). Nearly all of the complicated movements used by Swiss watch companies originate in this valley, about 30 miles north of Geneva. Audemars Piguet, Jaeger-LeCoultre and Breguet are headquartered in the Vallée de Joux and Blancpain does all its manufacturing there. Other companies, including Vacheron Constantin, Patek Philippe and Gérald Genta/Daniel Roth have manufacturing facilities there (these companies' headquarters

are in Geneva). The valley is also home to the move-ment makers Frédéric Piguet and Dubois Dépraz.

What town in Germany was a watchmaking center in the 19th century and has recently experienced a horological revival?

Glashütte. Located in the former East Germany, south of Dresden, the small town of Glashütte became one of Germany's most important watch centers when Ferdinand Adolph Lange founded a watch company (A. Lange & Söhne) there in 1845. The town's fortunes declined in the 20th century, thanks to war and decades of communism (in 1951, all the town's watch factories were blended into a single socialist combine). After the reunification of Germany, in 1990, watch-industry investors began to gravitate to Glashütte once again. Present-day Glashütte watch companies include A. Lange & Söhne (which has been re-established), Glashütte Original, Mühle-Glashütte and Nomos.

What city was a refuge for Protestant French watchmakers during the Reformation, and hence became a major watchmaking center?

Geneva, Switzerland. When Catholics were persecut-ing Protestants in France in the 16th century, many Protestants fled to Geneva, which the reformer Jean Calvin had converted into a staunchly Protestant city. Among these displaced French Protestants, also known as Huguenots, were many watchmakers from French watchmaking cities such as Paris and Blois.

Where is the world's most important watch indus-try exhibition held each year?

In Basel, Switzerland. Every spring, exhibitors representing more than 300 watch brands converge on this city in the northwest of the country to show their goods to some 90,000 store buyers and other visitors.

Where in Switzerland are watch movements tested before receiving certification as chronometers?
In Bienne, Le Locle and Geneva. COSC, the Swiss agency that tests chronometers, has facilities in each of these cities.

Where in Japan did that country's watch industry originate?
Osaka. The first Japanese watch manufacturer, Osaka Watch Co., was founded there in 1889. The company survived only until 1902, but the watch industry that developed in its wake became one of the watchmaking world's superpowers.

What region is the world's biggest watch assembler?
Hong Kong/southern China. Hong Kong-based watch companies, nearly all with factories in southern China, assemble roughly 1 billion watches per year, using movements from Japanese-, Swiss-, and Chinese-owned firms. Because the vast majority of the region's companies don't make movements, Hong Kong is usually referred to as an assembly center rather than a production center like Japan or Switzerland.

Seiko is closely associated with one of the best-known landmarks in Tokyo. What is it?
The Hattori Clock Tower atop the Wako department store in the fashionable Ginza district. The store, which is owned by Seiko, stands on the site where Seiko Watch Corp. founder Kintaro Hattori opened a prestigious watch and clock shop in 1895.

What town is considered to be the birthplace of the American watch industry?

Waltham, Massachusetts. That's where, in 1850, Aaron Dennison and Edward Howard founded America's first watch company, which after several name changes became the Waltham Watch Co. The company was in business for a century and produced some 35 million watches.

Where is Time Day celebrated?
Japan. The holiday, observed each year on June 10, is intended to remind Japanese of the importance of spending time wisely. The first Time Day was celebrated in 1920. The holiday has roughly the same importance in Japan as Flag Day or Groundhog Day does in the United States.

Throughout most of his professional life, Abraham-Louis Breguet lived in the same neighborhood, surrounded by some of the greatest watchmakers of his time. What neighborhood was it?
The western part of the Île de la Cité in Paris. Breguet's house was in a row of homes and workshops along the Seine whose many watchmaker inhabitants earned it the name Quai de l'Horloge, or "clock embankment." Breguet's neighbors included Jean-Antoine Lépine, Ferdinand and Louis Berthoud and Pierre Le Roy.

In the 18th and 19th centuries, what Swiss village was best known for making watches sold in China?
Fleurier, a remote village in the Jura Mountains. Initially, watches made for China, a very large market for luxury timepieces, differed from other watches only in their degree of decoration: the Chinese liked a great deal of enameling and pearls. Eventually, elaborate decoration extended to the movements as well, with bridges and plates engraved or engine-

turned. The best-known Fleurier company was Bovet, founded in 1820 by Édouard Bovet.

Both Seiko and Citizen have factories in the Japanese Alps. Why?

Both companies opened factories in the mountains in Nagano Prefecture, a relatively remote region west of Tokyo, during World War II because it was safe from Allied bombing. The Tokyo factories of both companies were damaged by bombs.

Where is Plan-les-Ouates and what is its connection to watches?

It is an industrial area on the outskirts of Geneva that in recent years has become a Mecca for high-end watch companies. Since 1997, Patek Philippe, Vacheron Constantin, Rolex, Piaget. Frédérique Constant and de Grisogono have all built factories and/or headquarters there.

STYLE AND DESIGN

Who designed a watch for Movado that had five separate cases?
Andy Warhol. In 1988, the year after Warhol's death, Movado introduced a watch called Andy Warhol Times/5, the first in its Artists Collection of watches. The watch consisted of five rectangular cases, each containing a quartz movement, linked together to form a bracelet. Each watch face bore a different black-and-white photo, taken by Warhol, of New York City streets and buildings.

What watch made waves in 1972 because it was the first luxury watch with a steel case?
The Royal Oak, by Audemars Piguet. Designed by Gérald Genta, it sported a porthole-shaped, riveted bezel and was built in massive proportions (massive, that is, for its time, when watches were generally smaller than they are today). It sold for 3,330 Swiss francs. Since then, steel has become the most popular metal for luxury watches (as it is for watches in all price categories).

What is a "grand guichet"?

The term is French for "big window" (specifically, a window like those in banks and post offices) and it refers to a date display composed of a large, rectangular aperture, often divided by a bar, that shows the numeral(s) of the day of the month.

To what watch-face feature does the term "Cyclops eye" refer?
A small magnifying lens, incorporated into the watch crystal, that makes the date on a calendar watch easier to read. Rolex patented the lens in 1952. The concept is now used by many brands.

The designer of the famous Hamilton Electric Ventura also designed cars, vacuum cleaners and dirigibles. Who was he?
Richard Arbib. The designer had a penchant for fins and wing-like projections, which can be seen in his designs not just for the futuristic Ventura and other Hamilton Electric models, but also for automobiles, boats and appliances. One of the cars he designed, the Astra-Gnome, appeared on the cover of *Newsweek* in 1956. Toward the end of his life (he died in 1995), Arbib became convinced that dirigibles were due for a comeback and spent much time sketching new designs for them in preparation for the revival.

The watch brand Hublot is credited with starting the fashion for what watch design feature?
Rubber straps. The story goes that before the brand's introduction, Hublot's founder, Carlo Crocco, was examining renderings for the new watches and admired the plain black straps that had been sketched merely as stand-ins for the not-yet-designed actual straps. He liked them so much, in fact, that he decided to realize them using a simple, supple material: black rubber. In 1980, contrary to the

advice of nearly everyone around him, he introduced his new brand featuring the unlikely combination of 18-karat-gold cases and rubber straps.

What well-known watchmaker of a bygone era is known as the father of modern watch design?
Abraham-Louis Breguet. He eschewed the 18th-century vogue for elaborate decoration, choosing simplicity instead, and replaced the bulky cases that prevailed at the time with slim, sleek ones.

What is a "regulator" dial?
A dial in which the hours and seconds are indicated on separate subdials rather than on the main center dial. The purpose is to make the minutes hand, mounted in the center, easier to read. The name "regulator" comes from the fact that the large pendulum clocks once used to regulate the time in watch factories and celestial observatories had this type of dial.

What was the theme of the well-known "One More Time" collection of Swatches, designed by the artist Alfred Hofkunst?
Food. The three watches, introduced in 1991, were inspired by a cucumber, a chili pepper, and bacon and eggs. They were carried only by upscale food stores and sold out in three hours.

What are "Breguet" hands?
Watch hands decorated with hollow circles near the tips. They are named for the great watchmaker Abraham-Louis Breguet (1747-1823), who used them because he thought them easier to read than the extremely ornate hands found on many watches of his time.

Who were Skeezix, Smitty and Rudy Nebb?

Comic strip characters who adorned some of the earliest character watches, which first appeared in the late 1920s. The most famous character watch, Ingersoll's Mickey Mouse, was introduced in 1933.

What watch did the famous photographer Edward Steichen declare to be the only "really original and beautiful" watch he had ever seen?

The watch, designed in 1947, that came to be known as the Museum Watch. Steichen made the statement in a letter to the watch's designer, Nathan George Horwitt. The design, which was inspired by the Bauhaus movement, consisted of a simple metallic dot (the first prototypes had both golden and silver-colored ones, though in later versions only gold-colored ones were used), a black face without markers and two hands. Steichen was director of the photography department at the Museum of Modern Art, which in 1960 accepted a prototype of the watch for exhibition. It was produced not by Movado, which did not yet own the design, but by Vacheron Constantin and LeCoultre. Movado bought the design from Horwitt soon afterward. Horwitt had great difficulty selling his design; many watch companies rejected it before its purchase by Movado.

What does "guilloché" mean?

It's French for a type of watch-dial decoration consisting of fine, wavy lines engraved by machine. "Engine-turned" is a synonym for "guilloché."

What are "côtes de Genève"?

Translated literally as "Geneva ribbing" but more often as "Geneva waves" or "Geneva stripes," the term refers to the decorative striped pattern sometimes used on movement plates and bridges.

Who designed Omega's Constellation and Seamaster models, Patek Philippe's Nautilus and Golden Ellipse, and the Royal Oak by Audemars Piguet?
Gérald Genta. A watch designer since 1952, Genta is a well-known figure in the watch industry with a reputation for innovative designs. Among the design ideas he has popularized are retrograde displays and the use of unorthodox materials such as carbon fiber.

What is a "jump-hour" display?
A display that shows the hour by means of a numeral in an aperture rather than a hand rotating around a dial. In some jump-hour watches, the minutes are shown via an additional aperture; in others, they are indicated in the standard rotating-hand manner.

What famous designer did Bulova recruit to design the case for its Accutron watch?
Raymond Loewy, the famous industrial designer and champion of the streamline-design movement. After hiring him, Bulova did not like his designs and assigned in-house personnel to come up with nearly all those that were ultimately used for the Accutron, which was introduced in 1960.

In what decade did the trend emerge of using indexes instead of numerals on watch dials?
The 1930s. They had been used occasionally before then, usually in combination with numerals, but a new interest in simple watch dials in the 1930s made indexes far more prevalent.

What is a "form" watch?
Any watch that is not round. The term "form movement" refers to any movement that is not round.

What company is credited with triggering the

plastic-and-diamonds fashion that swept the watch industry in 2000?
Technomarine, which in 1999 introduced a watch called TechnoDiamond, a divers' watch with a plastic strap and steel case set with diamonds. The watch was a hit with celebrities and inspired many other companies to introduce watches made of the same unlikely combination of materials.

What is "perlage"?
A way of decorating a movement plate or other surface, such as a dial, with a pattern of close-together or overlapping circles composed of concentric lines. It is also called "circular graining." The technique gets its name from the circles' resemblance to pearls ("perles" in French).

What do the words "dauphine," "baton" and "feuille" refer to?
Different styles of watch hands. Dauphine hands are shaped like elongated triangles, with the tip pointing to the hour or minute; baton hands are straight their entire length, like an unsharpened pencil; and feuille (French for "leaf") hands are pointed at both ends and thickest in the middle.

What is a "cloche" watch?
A watch shaped like a cowbell ("cloche" is French for "bell"). The company best known for this type of watch is Cartier, which made cloche watches in the 1920s.

What are "Vendôme" lugs?
Lugs (metal appendages used to attach the watch strap to the case) that consist of T-shaped bars affixed to the case at the 12 and 6 o'clock positions. One well-known watch with such lugs is the Cartier Pasha.

What is a "tonneau" watch?
A watch shaped like a barrel, i.e., having convex
vertical sides. "Tonneau" is French for "barrel." The
name was coined by Cartier.

What is a "tortue" watch?
Similar to a tonneau, a tortue watch is shaped like a
turtle shell, meaning its vertical sides are convex.
"Tortue" is French for "tortoise." The name was
coined by Cartier.

WATCHES AND CRIME

What famous criminal owned a very rare Rolex Prince auctioned off by Sotheby's after his death in 1947?
Al Capone. The watch, reference 3140, was made in 1937, and featured Arabic numerals, blued steel hands, and hooded lugs. When Capone died following a stroke in 1947, his son consigned the watch to Sotheby's.

A videotape of Osama bin Laden released in the weeks after Sept. 11, 2001 was widely believed to show him wearing what watch?
A Timex. Media outlets including MSNBC identified a watch seen in one of bin Laden's videotapes as a Timex digital. (Jay Leno aired a comic segment about the watch on the *Tonight Show* on Oct. 11.) Later, Timex said that after examining the tape closely it had determined the watch was not a Timex after all. The watch's real maker has not been identified.

In the 17th century, a watch was an accomplice in what attempted regicide?
Guy Fawkes's attempt to kill James I and his ministers in the famous Gunpowder Plot. Fawkes intended to

blow up the Palace of Westminster, and the king along with it, on Nov. 5, 1605, but was apprehended before he could set off the gunpowder he and his fellow plotters had placed in the cellar of the building. On his person, the authorities found a watch that had been lent to him by co-conspirator Thomas Percy. Just what Fawkes intended to do with it is unclear (watches were extremely imprecise at the time, and not very useful). One historian says he meant to use it to time the burning of the fuse that would ignite the gunpowder; others say he needed a way to keep track of the hours so he would know when his intended victims were in harm's way.

What watch was the notorious bank robber Clyde Barrow carrying when he and Bonnie Parker were gunned down in 1934?
An Elgin pocket watch.

In 1983 one of the most famous watches ever made was stolen from a museum in Jerusalem. What watch was it?
The so-called "Marie Antoinette" watch, made by the company founded by the great watchmaker Abraham-Louis Breguet. The watch, the most complicated of its time, was nicknamed the "Marie Antoinette" because it was made at the request of one of the officers of her guard as a gift for her. The queen never saw the watch: it was only completed in 1827, 34 years after her death. The Marie Antoinette and many others once owned by the engineer and watch collector Sir David Lionel Salomons were stolen from Jerusalem's L.A. Mayer Memorial Institute for Islamic Art, to which they had been bequeathed. The watch has not been recovered.

Whom did British police publicly praise for his

bravery during a watch theft in November 2004?

Rocker and TV star Ozzy Osbourne. Around 4 a.m. on Nov. 22, 2004, an intruder stole 2 million pounds' (about $3.6 million) worth of jewelry and watches from Osbourne's estate in Buckinghamshire after a birthday celebration there for Elton John's close friend David Furnish. Osbourne tackled the burglar but did not prevent his jumping out of a first floor window and escaping with several expensive pieces of jewelry and two Franck Muller watches. One of the watches belonged to a limited series of 10 pieces. Police praised Osbourne for his courage in taking on the thief. (The Osbournes' bad watch luck didn't end there. Just three months later, 19-year-old son Jack had three watches, a Franck Muller, a Rolex and a Harry Winston, stolen from his luggage during a trip from Los Angeles to London.)

In 1994, 28 watches were stolen from the Deutschses Museum in Munich. What was note-worthy about them?

Many were "erotic" watches, i.e., they belonged to a genre of watches that graphically depict sexual acts by means of moving figures, often hidden underneath the watch's cover. The watches were part of a traveling exhibit organized by the Blancpain watch company. The watches were recovered, many of them badly damaged from mishandling, in 1998.

What famous musician had one of his Breguet watches stolen from a hotel room in New York?

Arthur Rubinstein. He owned several Breguets, one of which was stolen from his room in the Waldorf Astoria when he was on a concert tour.

A watchmaker named Robert Hubert was hanged in London in the 17th century for a crime he did

not commit. What crime was it?
Starting the Great Fire of London. Hubert, who was
mentally handicapped, falsely confessed to setting
London on fire at the behest of the pope and was
hanged at Tyburn. (At the time there was much anti-
Catholicism in England and an eagerness to blame
the disaster on Rome.) It turned out that the fire
actually began at a baker's shop in Pudding Lane,
where a maid had neglected to put out the oven fire
before going to bed.

**Cat burglar Bill Mason, who described his 30-year
career in the book *Confessions of a Master Jewel
Thief*, once stole a watch from Phyllis Diller. What
watch was it?**
A Cartier given her by Bob Hope. It was part of some
$300,000 worth of jewelry Mason stole from Diller.

**In the 1950s a world-famous athlete had his
extremely valuable Patek Philippe stolen after
owning it for less than a year. Who was it?**
The boxer Sugar Ray Robinson. He bought the
watch, a pink-gold chronograph with perpetual
calendar, in January 1957, only to have it stolen in
September while on a trip to Italy.

**Why were 100,000 watches destroyed in Switzer-
land on Aug. 11, 2004?**
They were counterfeit. The Swiss customs office, aided
by the Federation of the Swiss Watch Industry,
destroyed the watches (weighing more than 5 tons) by
placing them in a shredder. Swiss customs officials
had seized the watches over a 5-year period. Although
such actions have taken place in other countries, the
shredding, in the canton of Fribourg, was the first
mass destruction of counterfeit watches to take place
in Switzerland.

What watch museum was burglarized twice in less than two years?

The Museum of Watchmaking and Enameling in Geneva. The first break-in was on Aug. 31, 2001, when thieves stole about $1.3 million worth of timepieces and jewelry. The second burglary occurred Nov. 24, 2002. In it, the burglars affixed a pole to a truck and used it as a battering ram to break through the museum's doors, making off with some $670,000 worth of items.

How did a Rolex watch lead to the capture of a famous Canadian con man and murderer in the 1990s?

The corpse of the victim, Ronald Platt, was identifiable only by the serial number of the Rolex watch on its wrist. The murderer, Albert Walker, was a Canadian swindler living in England who killed Platt after stealing his identity. Walker was apprehended after Platt's body was recovered from the English Channel in 1996, and police realized there were actually two Ronald Platts, one of them an imposter. The crime was the subject of a made-for-TV movie released in 2002 and a play, entitled *Stolen Lives: The Albert Walker Story*, by Canadian playwright Peter Colley.

A retired businessman named Stephen Morely filed a lawsuit involving a very famous, presumably stolen watch. What watch was it?

The Omega Speedmaster that astronaut Edwin "Buzz" Aldrin wore when he stepped onto the moon on July 20, 1969. The watch was the first to be worn on the moon (Neil Armstrong left his watch in the lunar module when he made his first step, moments before Aldrin did). In 1971, Aldrin tried to donate the watch, along with other space memorabilia, to the Smithsonian Institution, but the watch went missing from the package he sent to the museum and is thought to have been stolen. In 2003, Morely claimed he had the watch, and filed a lawsuit seeking to establish his ownership of it. He said he had bought it in 1991 for $175, not suspecting its exceptional provenance. (The woman who sold it to Morely told him that her father had found it on a California beach in the early 1970s.) In 2004, a judge in San Diego dismissed the case after the U.S. government concluded that the watch was not the one Aldrin wore after all.

WATCHES AND WRITERS

In 1901, Ingersoll, a forerunner of today's Timex Corp., received a letter that read, simply, "Dear Sir: Please send me a watch. $1 enclosed. Truly yours, _____." Who wrote the letter?

Mark Twain. He was requesting one of the company's famous Yankee pocket watches that sold for just $1 and gave rise to the slogan, "The Watch That Made the Dollar Famous." Nine days later, Twain wrote again, requesting a second Yankee, this time signing not his pen name but his real one. "$1 enclosed," he wrote. "Please send me another watch, obliged, Yours Truly, Samuel Clemens."

Who said, "Dictionaries are like watches. The worst is better than none, and the best cannot be expected to go quite true"?

Samuel Johnson, who in 1755 published *A Dictionary of the English Language*, the most authoritative English lexicon of its time.

In what work does the first known literary reference to a mechanical clock appear?

Dante's *Paradiso*, written between 1316 and 1321.

There are two references to clocks in the poem. The first, in Canto X, reads: "Then, as a clock tower calls us from above/when the Bride of God rises to sing her matins/to the Sweet Spouse, that she may earn his love…" The second reference, in Canto XXIV, reads: "As the wheels within a clockwork synchronize/so that the innermost, when looked at closely/seems to be standing, while the outermost flies…"

The same British writer who left us with a vivid eyewitness account of the 1666 Great Fire of London also detailed his fascination with his pocket watch. Who was it?

The diarist Samuel Pepys. In May 1665 he made one of many watch-related entries, writing, "I cannot forbear carrying my watch in my hand in the coach all this afternoon and seeing what [hour] it is 100 times. And am apt to think with myself: how could I be so long without one…"

A prominent author once published a piece in *The New Yorker* magazine describing the heartache she suffers one day when she believes her beloved wristwatch has been stolen. Who is the author and what watch causes her such anxiety?

The author is Muriel Spark, best known for her novel *The Prime of Miss Jean Brodie*, and the watch is a Cartier. Her 1997 article, entitled "My Watch, A True Story," recounts how she leaves her hexagonal, platinum-cased, diamond Cartier with a jeweler in Italy for repair and is told hours later that the watch has been stolen from the shop. In fact, the watch, dating from the 1930s, has merely fallen into a drawer. In the panic-filled interval before it is found, Spark learns that the watch she believed common-place is worth many thousands of dollars and, if recovered, must henceforth be kept under lock and key. She ends the story by noting, wistfully, "Back in the safety deposit box goes my friend, the watch, from which I've derived so much pleasure for the best part of my life. Nevermore do I leave it knocking around on my bedside table, or my desk, or on the side of the washbasin. Nevermore, nevermore."

What author insisted that a reporter who was interviewing him accept his Cartier watch as a gift, instructing him to "take off that awful watch and put this on"?

Truman Capote. During the meeting, in 1972, Capote learned that it was the reporter's (Gerald Clarke's) birthday and insisted on giving him the $1,600 watch, explaining that he wouldn't miss it because he had lots of watches. (The writer John Knowles, a friend of Capote, later told Clarke that Capote in fact had seven other watches "just like" the one he gave Clarke.) Clarke sent the watch back to Capote three days later with a note of gratitude. (Clarke later wrote a biography of Capote, which was published in 1988.)

In his will, a famous 19th-century novelist left to a longtime friend two treasured possessions: his manuscripts and his favorite watch. What novelist was it?

Charles Dickens. The will, signed in 1869, left to his biographer and close friend John Forster the watch and "manuscripts of my published works as may be in my possession at the time of my decease." Dickens died the next year. He had been given the watch, a gold repeater "of special construction," as Forster writes, at a public dinner in Coventry in 1858. The watch, made by the town's watchmakers, was a gift thanking him for his support for Coventry's technical school. According to Forster, Dickens "kept faithfully his pledge to the givers, that it should be thenceforward the inseparable companion of his workings and wanderings, and reckon off the future labours of his days until he should have done with the measurement of time."

Who said, "'Tis with our judgments as our watches, none/Go just alike, yet each believes his own"?
The British poet and satirist Alexander Pope, in "An Essay on Criticism," published in 1711.

What character in a famous work of fiction declares, "Oh dear! Oh dear! I shall be too late!" before pulling his watch out of his vest pocket?
The rabbit in Lewis Carroll's *Alice's Adventures in Wonderland* that Alice chases down the rabbit hole at the beginning of the book.

What writer and philosopher established a watchmaking community in Ferney, France?
Voltaire. Around 1770 he set up a group of workshops in Ferney, 4 miles from Geneva, to provide employment for Genevan watchmakers seeking refuge from the city's political oppression and violence. The watchmaking colony prospered, thanks in part to Voltaire's soliciting business from his acquaintances among the aristocracy of Europe. In 1878, a century after Voltaire's death, the French government renamed the town Ferney-Voltaire, which is its name today.

What Enlightenment writer and intellectual was descended from three generations of watchmakers and, as a child, pretended to be a watchmaker while playing with his grandfather's tools?
Jean-Jacques Rousseau. In his *Confessions* he wrote: "We [Rousseau and his cousin] spoiled the tools of my good old grandfather trying to make watches as

he did." In Rousseau's youth, his family considered having him trained as a watchmaker, but he had other ideas.

A watch figures prominently in the short story "The Gift of the Magi" by O. Henry. How?
The story is about an impoverished husband and wife who sell their most precious possessions to buy each other Christmas gifts. Unbeknownst to his wife, the husband sells his gold watch to buy her a set of expensive hair combs. In the meantime, unbeknownst to her husband, the wife sells her knee-length hair to a wig maker to buy her spouse a platinum chain for his treasured watch.

A 2002 exhibit at the Imperial War Museum in London featuring poets who fought in World War I included a watch owned by the English poet Edward Thomas. Why was the watch noteworthy?
It supposedly stopped running when jolted by the impact of the exploding shell that killed Thomas on Easter Day, April 9, 1917 in the Battle of Arras. Thomas, who was born in 1878, began his career writing prose, turned to verse in 1914, and influenced the work of W.H. Auden and Philip Larkin.

In what famous American novel does a lawyer say this about his watch (and his car): "When I buy an Ingersoll watch, or a Ford, I get a better tool for less money, and I know precisely what I am getting"?
Babbitt, by Sinclair Lewis, published in 1922. The lawyer is Seneca Doane, a supporter of labor unions and champion of various anti-Republican causes, who appears periodically as a foil to the conservative conformity ridiculed in the novel. The book also contains a remark by the main character, George

Babbitt, about his own watch-wearing habits. "I've never worn a wristwatch," he declares, proud of having resisted the newfangled gadgets that were just then, in the early 1920s, gaining acceptance by American men.

What Jules Verne character, finding himself poor, hungry and friendless in Japan, decides he would rather starve than sell his watch?
Jean Passepartout in *Around the World in Eighty Days*. His watch is a precious legacy from his great-grandfather.

One character in Jules Verne's novel *Around the World in Eighty Days* has an unshakeable belief in the infallibility of his watch. How does he demonstrate this conviction?
As the character, Jean Passepartout, and his employer, Phileas Fogg, circumnavigate the globe, Passepartout refuses to adjust his watch to the local times. When another character suggests he regulate his watch each day at noon so it will agree with the sun, he indignantly refuses: "I regulate my watch? Never!…So much the worse for the sun, monsieur. The sun will be wrong, then!"

What fictional character is so unflappable and so regular in his daily habits that the author compares him to a chronometer made by Pierre Le Roy or Thomas Earnshaw?
Phileas Fogg, the hero of *Around the World in Eighty Days*, by Jules Verne. (In at least one English translation of the book, Earnshaw's name is omitted and Fogg is compared only to a Le Roy.)

In Patrick O'Brian's historical novel, *Blue at the Mizzen*, a group of seamen discuss the standard

punishment meted out in the Royal Navy to perpetrators of a certain clock-related crime. What is the crime and how is it punished?

The crime is opening a marine chronometer's case. Due to the crime's potentially disastrous consequence, being lost at sea, the opening of a chronometer case by unauthorized seamen was punishable by death. In the novel, the ship's armourer's mate explains to the ship's surgeon: "You must understand, sir…that if you go for to open a time-keeper's case, by the Articles of War, you are flogged to death, your pay and allowances are forfeit, your widow has no pension, and you are buried with no words said over you."

In Shakespeare's time, before the invention of the pendulum and balance spring, clocks and watches were notoriously unreliable. In what play does Shakespeare compare a woman's behavior to the chronic errancy of a timepiece?

Love's Labour's Lost. He compares a watch's poor timekeeping to the stubborn foolishness of a woman who refuses to return the love of her ardent admirer. In act 3, scene 1, the character Biron compares Rosaline, the woman he loves unrequitedly, to a clock he hopes will eventually "go right." Rosaline, he says, "is like a German clock,/Still a-repairing; ever out of frame,/And never going a right, being a watch;/But being watch'd, that it may still go right!"

In a 1638 comedy, the playwright Richard Brome makes reference to the then astronomically high cost of watches. What play was it?

The Antipodes, or, *The World Turned Upside Down*. The play depicts life in the antipodes, the imaginary region on the other side of the earth where everything is the opposite of what it is in the world we know.

Along with honest lawyers, old schoolboys and women who fight duels, the antipodes contains watches so cheap everyone can afford them, or, as Brome writes: "Every puny clerk can carry the time of day in his pocket."

What fictional character taken into custody in a foreign land mystifies his captors by showing them a watch, an instrument they had never seen before? Lemuel Gulliver, of *Gulliver's Travels*, by Jonathan Swift. When he is being held captive in Lilliput, his tiny tormenters ask him to empty his pockets so they can take an inventory of his possessions and present it to their emperor. They write the following about his watch, whose purpose they can't discern: "He put this engine to our ears, which made an incessant noise like that of a watermill: and we conjecture that it is either some unknown animal, or the god he worships, but we are more inclined to the latter opinion, because he assures us…that he seldom did anything without consulting it: he called it his oracle, and said it pointed out the time for every action of his life."

The 17ᵗʰ century biographer John Aubrey, whose notes and incidental writings were compiled in a book called *Aubrey's Brief Lives*, tells the story of a chambermaid who throws a watch, owned by a certain Thomas Allen, out a window. Why does she do it? (Hint: It is not so she can see time fly.) She believes the watch is possessed by the devil. The incident occurs at the house of a friend whom Allen (1542–1632) is visiting, in an era when watches are all but unknown. Allen, who is an astrologer (consulted by Queen Elizabeth I, among others), is believed by some to have magical powers. During his visit, he leaves his watch unattended on a windowsill. A chambermaid hears it ticking and concludes it is a demon. Using a pair of tongs, she picks it up by the chain and hurls it out the window, hoping it will land in the moat surrounding the house. Instead, the chain gets stuck on a tree branch–providing further evidence of the watch's infernal nature–and Allen is able to recover it.

What watch does Dirk Pitt, hero of many best-selling adventure novels by Clive Cussler, wear?
A Doxa diving watch with an orange dial. Pitt's creator first came face to face with the watch, which Doxa introduced in 1966, when he was supporting himself by working in a diving-equipment store while writing his first novel.

What famous French playwright was an eminent watchmaker and the inventor of a type of escapement?
Beaumarchais, né Pierre-Augustin Caron (1732-1799). His most famous works were *The Marriage of Figaro* and *The Barber of Seville*, upon which Mozart and Rossini, respectively, based celebrated operas. At age 21, Caron, who was the son of a Paris clockmaker, invented the double virgule escapement, which he boasted allowed him to make watches as thin as anyone could possibly want without sacrificing quality (thin watches were then very much in vogue in France). His fellow watchmaker Jean-André Lepaute tried to claim the invention as his own, but the French Academy of Sciences ruled in Caron's favor. Thanks to his victory, Caron won the attention and admiration of the royal court. Despite his success there (he made watches for Madame de Pompadour and Louis XV, among others), he ultimately gave up watchmaking and in 1767 began writing for the stage. (He had started calling himself "Beaumarchais" in 1757, naming himself after an estate owned by his

wife. In 1761 he became a nobleman when a friend purchased for him a position as royal secretary at court, and thus obtained a legal right to the Beaumarchais name.) He completed *The Barber of Seville* in 1773 and *The Marriage of Figaro* in 1778. (One interesting note: Beaumarchais was the brother-in-law of the famous French watchmaker Jean-Antoine Lépine, who married Beaumarchais's sister, Madeleine-Françoise.)

Whose story does the best-selling book, *Longitude*, tell?

That of John Harrison, who in the 18th century developed the first chronometer accurate enough to be used for marine navigation. The book, by Dava Sobel, was published in 1995.

An Italian villa owned by one prominent watch executive was featured on the cover of the best-selling novel *Under the Tuscan Sun*, by Frances Mayes. Who is the executive?

Luigi "Gino" Macaluso, owner of the Sowind Group, the holding company for the Girard-Perregaux and JeanRichard brands and the movement-making company GP Manufacture SA. Macaluso, an architect by training, also owns four villas in La Chaux-de-Fonds, three of which are used for his company's operations.

In John Synge's play *The Playboy of the Western World*, the character Jimmy Farrell describes a timepiece-related death. What exactly caused the death?

Ingestion of a clock movement. Farrell makes the reference while discussing insanity with another character, the widow Quin. "It's a fright, surely," Farrell says. "I knew a party was kicked in the head by a red mare, and he went killing horses a great while, till he eat the insides of a clock and died after."

In the 1963 Ian Fleming novel *On Her Majesty's Secret Service*, James Bond breaks his watch and has to get a new one. How does he break it?

He uses the watch, a "heavy Rolex Oyster Perpetual with expanding metal bracelet," as brass knuckles and smashes the watch's face against that of his enemy. Fleming writes: "Bond's right [hand] flashed out and the face of the Rolex disintegrated against the man's jaw." Later, Bond realizes he must replace the watch: "Bond lifted his left wrist. Remembered that he no longer had a watch. That he would certainly be allowed on expenses. He would get another one as soon as the shops opened after Boxing Day. Another Rolex? Probably. They were on the heavy side, but they worked. And at least you could see the time in the dark with those big phosphorus numerals."

In Ian Fleming's *From Russia, with Love* (1956), the KGB assassin Donovan Grant wears a watch from what company?

Girard-Perregaux. At the very beginning of the book, Fleming describes the "typical membership badges of the rich man's club" to which Grant belongs. They include a Dunhill lighter, a gold Fabergé cigarette case and "a bulky gold wristwatch on a well-used brown crocodile strap." Fleming continues: "It was a Girard-Perregaux model designed for people who like gadgets, and it had a sweep second-hand and two little windows in the face to tell the day of the month, and the month, and the phase of the moon. The story it told now was 2:30 on June 10 with the moon three-quarters full." Later, the novel's hero, James Bond, whose own, unnamed watch has been de-stroyed by a bullet from a gun disguised as a book, confiscates Grant's watch after killing him on a train: "Bond looked at Nash's watch ["Nash" is one of Grant's aliases], which was now on his own wrist. 4:30. Another hour to Dijon."

What famous book about evolution has the word "watchmaker" in its title?

The Blind Watchmaker, a book about natural selection written by Oxford zoologist Richard Dawkins and published in 1986. The book's title is meant as a refutation of the idea, put forth by the 18th and early 19th-century theologian William Paley, that the universe must have been created by a "divine watch-maker" because it appears to be so carefully planned. Dawkins explains that species are not created from a grand plan but through automatic, inexorable processes. Dawkins writes, "It [natural selection] has no vision, no foresight, no sight at all. If it can be said to play the role of watchmaker in nature, it is the *blind* watchmaker."

What character from a Victorian novel has so many watches that her apartments "are alive with their clicking"?

Becky Crawley, née Sharp, in William Makepeace Thackeray's *Vanity Fair*, published in 1848. Two of her watches are gifts from her admirers and one is from her loutish husband, Rawdon Crawley. Thackeray writes: "Happening to mention one night that [her watch], which Rawdon had given her, was of English workmanship, and went ill, on the very next morning there came to her a little bijou marked Leroy, with a chain and cover charmingly set with turquoises, and another signed Breguet, which was covered with pearls, and yet scarcely bigger than a half-crown. General Tufto had bought one, and Captain Osborne had gallantly presented the other."

What writer penned these lines about a Breguet watch: "A dandy on the boulevards/Strolling at leisure/Until his Breguet, ever vigilant,/Reminds him it is midday"?

Alexander Pushkin, in his verse novel *Eugene Onegin*, written between 1825 and 1831 and considered to be the poet's masterpiece. The "dandy" is the title character, an idle and frivolous aristocrat. In Pushkin's time, Breguet watches were status symbols among the nobility of many European countries, including Russia. (Pushkin's own father, a count, owned a Breguet repeating watch.) Onegin's Breguet tells him when it is time to move from one diversion to the next, from leisurely stroll to Champagne-drenched dinner to lavish ballet.

What writer makes the following observation: "Breguet makes a watch which for 20 years never goes wrong, while the wretched machine inside which we pass our existence goes wrong and produces aches and pains at least once a week"?

Stendhal, in a piece called "Rome, Naples and Florence," published in 1817.

What celebrated 19ᵗʰ-century French writer makes references to Breguet watches in three novels?

Honoré de Balzac. He mentions Breguet watches in three novels in the *Comédie Humaine* series: *Le Père Goriot*, *Eugénie Grandet* and *La Rabouilleuse*. In the last of these, Balzac shows that he has at least a passing acquaintance with the technical achievements of the great watchmaker. He refers to one of his inventions, a ratchet key, which came to be known as a "Breguet key," designed to prevent winding in the wrong direction: "A fine gold chain hung from the pocket of his waistcoat, where a flat watch could just be seen. He toyed with the 'ratchet' key, which

Breguet had just invented." (Another translation refers to the key as a "locust" key, another name for ratchet key.) Breguet had actually invented the key sometime around 1789, long before the scene in the novel, which occurs in 1821.

What author wrote a novella in which a Russian prince gives away his Breguet repeater watch?

Leo Tolstoy. In *Hadji Murat*, which takes place in 1851, during the Russian conquest of the Caucasus, Prince Vorontsov makes a good-will gift of his Breguet to a Chechen defector, the title character, who has joined the Russian side of the conflict. Tolstoy writes: "Vorontsov took out his Breguet watch and pressed the spring. The watch struck quarter past four. Hadji Murat was evidently intrigued by the striking of the watch and asked if Vorontsov would make it strike again and allow him to see it." Vorontsov, whose young son has just received an expensive dagger as a gift from Hadji Murat, then gives the Chechen the watch in gratitude for his generosity. "He [Hadji Murat] put his hand to his heart and took it," Tolstoy writes. "He pressed the spring a few times, listened and shook his head approvingly." In a later scene, he again listens to the repeater, while "suppressing a childish smile," and an onlooker assures him that it is a good watch given to him by a good man.

What novel is centered on the real-world theft of Breguet's "Marie Antoinette" watch from a museum in Jerusalem?

The Grand Complication, by Allen Kurzweil, published in 2001. It's about the efforts of an eccentric, elderly collector and a young librarian to find the stolen watch, the most complicated watch of its time. The timepiece was ordered as a gift for Marie Antoinette by a member of her guard but only completed decades after her death. In April 1983 it was stolen from the L.A. Mayer Memorial Museum for Islamic Art in Jerusalem and never recovered.

What poet wrote about using an astrolabe to regulate clocks?
Geoffrey Chaucer. He made the reference in "A Treatise on the Astrolabe," written in 1391. (The astrolabe was a navigational instrument used to determine the altitude of celestial bodies.) Chaucer wrote the work for his 10-year-old son, who was attending Oxford. It was the first English-language treatise on a scientific instrument.

WHAT'S IN A NAME?

Most watch companies are named after their founders (Breguet, Patek Philippe, Bulova, Vacheron Constantin, etc.) or their locations (Elgin, Waltham, IWC Schaffhausen, and so on). Some names, though, come from other sources. What are the origins of the following watch company and/or brand names?

Citizen
The name was coined by the then mayor of Tokyo, Shinpei Goto, and first used in 1924. Goto was a friend of Kamekichi Yamazaki, a Tokyo jeweler who had in 1918 opened a watch factory to make modestly priced pocket watches for the Japanese market. Yamazaki asked the mayor to suggest a name for his new watches, and Goto came up with "Citizen," which he believed connoted affordability because it suggested the watches were within the grasp of all citizens.

Doxa
The name means "glory," "honor," "magnificence" or "praise" in Greek.

Fossil

The company was named for the father of Tom and Kosta Kartsotis, Fossil Inc.'s chairman and president, respectively. (Tom Kartsotis and three others founded the firm in 1984 and were later joined by Kosta.) In their youth, the brothers teasingly referred to their father as "The Old Fossil."

Hamilton

The company was named after Andrew Hamilton, founder of the town of Lancaster, Pennsylvania, where Hamilton Watch Co. came into being in 1892. Andrew Hamilton was a prominent lawyer in colonial America who served as attorney general of Pennsylvania. He was also an architect, designing Independence Hall in Philadelphia.

Hublot

The name is French for "porthole." It refers to the bezel of the brand's first and best-known model, which is studded with tiny screws that make it look like a porthole.

Minerva

The company and brand were named after the Roman goddess of wisdom, who was also the patroness of arts and crafts (and presumably would have presided over watchmaking, if it had existed in ancient Roman times).

Movado

The name, first used in 1905, means "always in motion" in the universal language of Esperanto.

Pulsar

The Pulsar, the world's first digital watch, was named for a type of celestial object that emits bursts of energy at extremely precise intervals ("pulsar" is short for "pulsating star"). The name was chosen because the watch had a time display that lit up briefly in bright digits when the wearer pressed a button; these "energy pulses" were analogous to those of a pulsar. Furthermore, the watch had a quartz movement (a rarity in 1972, when the Pulsar was launched by Hamilton Watch Co.), making it extremely precise, like a pulsating star. In the beginning, the name applied to the watch alone, but later came to denote an entire watch brand, now owned by Seiko Corp.

Seiko
In Japanese, *seiko* means both "precision manufacturing" and "success." The name dates back to 1892, when Kintaro Hattori, a clock dealer and repairer, bought a glass factory, converted it to clock production, and named it "Seikosha" (*sha* is Japanese for "house"). The first watch to carry the name "Seiko" was introduced in 1924.

Swatch
The name is a contraction of "Swiss" and "watch." The Swatch brand was launched in 1982. In 1998 the name of the brand's parent company was changed from SMH (Société Suisse Microélectronique et d'Horlogerie) to the Swatch Group in honor of the brand.

Why is the "split seconds" chronograph so named?
The name refers to the two superimposed seconds hands that separate, or "split" apart, when the chronograph is used to time multiple events that begin simultaneously but end at different times, such as runners running a race. The two hands rotate together (one sits directly on top of the other so they appear to be one hand) until the first event ends–the

fastest runner crosses the finish line, for instance. At that point, one of the hands is stopped, so the first runner's time can be noted, while the other hand continues to run, timing the remaining runner or runners.

How did the chronograph get its name?
The name is a combination of the Greek words *chronos*, meaning "time," and *graphos*, meaning "something that writes." It dates back to an early form of chronograph whose center seconds hand was fitted with a tiny reservoir for holding ink. The hand could be pushed down on the dial to make a dot, thus recording the amount of elapsed time.

How did the Rolex Oyster get its name?
The name is meant to connote impermeability because oyster shells are so difficult to open. Legend has it that Rolex founder Hans Wilsdorf came up with the name when he was preparing oysters for a dinner party.

Although the name "ETA" looks like an acronym, it is really a contraction. Of what?
The watch company name "Eterna." ETA, now the largest movement maker in Switzerland, and part of the giant Swatch Group, started out in 1932 as the movement-making arm of Eterna SA, in Grenchen.

What does the acronym "COSC" stand for?
Contrôle officiel suisse des chronomètres, or Swiss Official Chronometer Testing Institute. COSC is the Swiss agency that tests and certifies chronometers.

"Fifty Fathoms," the name of a famous water-resistant watch by Blancpain, is a misnomer. Why?
Because the watch is actually water-resistant to about

110 fathoms, or 200 meters. (One fathom equals 6 feet, or about 1.8 meters.) When the watch was introduced, in 1953, it was guaranteed water-resistant to 50 fathoms, or about 92 meters.

What does the "TAG" in "TAG Heuer" stand for?

Techniques d'Avant-Garde, the company, owned by the Saudi Ojjeh family, that bought the watch firm Heuer in 1985. In 1999, TAG sold the TAG Heuer watch brand to the luxury goods giant LVMH, but the acronym "TAG" was retained.

What code name was given to the Swatch while it was being developed?

"Delirium Vulgare." The name is Latin for "Delirium for the common people," and refers to the fact that the Swatch, designed to sell for just $30 or so, was constructed in a way similar to the high-end Delirium watch. (Both were developed by the movement maker ETA.) The Swatch was also called "Popularis," another reference to its intended mass appeal.

What was Patek Philippe's original name?

Patek, Czapek & Co. The company was founded in 1839 by Antoine Norbert de Patek and François Czapek. Adrien Philippe later replaced Czapek as Patek's partner and the company was renamed.

Where does the name "Valjoux" come from?

It's a contraction of "Vallée de Joux," the valley in Switzerland's Jura Mountains famous for the complicated movements made there. The name refers to a series of mechanical movements manufactured by the Swatch Group's ETA subsidiary. (The company now stamps these movements "ETA," not "Valjoux," but the name is still used widely in the watch industry to refer to these calibers.) The most famous Valjoux movement is the 7750 automatic chronograph.

The well-known watch designer and entrepreneur Gérald Genta no longer markets his watch brand under the name "Gérald Genta." What name does he use?
Gérald Charles. In 1996, Genta sold his Gérald Genta brand, along with the right to use the Gérald Genta name on watches, to the Singapore company Hour Glass. In 2000, when Hour Glass sold the brand to Bulgari SA, Genta left the firm and launched another brand, substituting his middle name, Charles, for Genta.

If one of the founders of Baume & Mercier had not changed his name, what would the company now be called?
Baume & Tchereditchenko. Paul Mercier, a Russian who assumed Swiss nationality, was born Paul Tchereditchenko and took on his mother's maiden name sometime after he met William Baume in 1912. Baume and Mercier became partners in 1918.

In 1915, Hans Wilsdorf and his partner Alfred James Davis decided to change the name of their company, "Wilsdorf and Davis." Why?
The German name "Wilsdorf" had become a liability due to the anti-German feeling that prevailed in Britain, where the company was based, during World War I. The partners instead adopted the name "Rolex," which they had started using as a brand name on their watches shortly before war broke out in 1914. The exact source of the name "Rolex" is not known.

What's another name for a balance spring?
A hairspring. The name comes from the extreme

thinness of the spring, which regulates the oscillations of the balance wheel.

What does the name "Kif" refer to?
A brand of shock-resistance device, second in watch-industry fame to the Incabloc brand.

What modern-day watch executive was named after a watch brand?
Philippe Stern, chairman and owner of Patek Philippe. Stern's grandfather and great-uncle bought Patek Philippe in 1932 and later passed it on to Philippe Stern's father, Henri, who named Philippe in its honor.

AMERICANA

What U.S. retailing partners earned their living in the watch business before they became the owners of a well-known chain of stores?

Sears and Roebuck. Richard Sears, a railroad station agent in Minnesota, became a watch marketer in 1886 when he purchased an unwanted shipment of watches sent to a Minneapolis jeweler. Sears sold the watches to his fellow station agents, disposing of them so successfully that he ordered more, and later that year set up a company called the R.W. Sears Watch Co., in North Redwood, Minnesota. He moved his firm to Chicago the next year and hired watchmaker Alvah Roebuck, from Hammond, Indiana, to work for him. They formed the mail-order company Sears, Roebuck and Co. in 1893, first selling only watches and jewelry and then branching out into just about everything else. In 1895, they published a 532-page catalog featuring hats, guns, buggies, baby carriages and a vast range of other items.

One object in the Smithsonian Institution's National Museum of American History proves that Benjamin Franklin believed literally in the adage,

"Time is money." What object is it?
A half-dollar bill, designed by Franklin in 1776, which bears the picture of a sundial.

In the 1950s, Yankees slugger Mickey Mantle appeared in magazine ads for a U.S. watch brand. Which brand was it and what did the advertisements depict?
The brand was Timex. The ads showed Mantle hitting a baseball with a Timex strapped to his bat and claimed that he had hit 50 home runs in that manner with no ill effects on the watch. The ads were part of Timex's famous "takes a licking and keeps on ticking" campaign that depicted various "torture tests" to which the company subjected its watches to prove their durability.

What Swiss-born watch marketer launched a brand designed exclusively for the U.S. market?
Albert Wittnauer. Wittnauer emigrated to the United States in 1872 to work with his brother-in-law importing Longines watches from Switzerland. In 1880, he introduced the Wittnauer brand to meet U.S. demand for a line that was similar to Longines but lower in price.

The U.S. company Bulova introduced its most famous watch in 1960. What was it called?
The Accutron. The watch, which ran on a battery, had a tuning-fork-shaped oscillator that made it the most accurate watch of its time, gaining or losing no more than a minute a month. In its heyday it was the most popular $100-plus watch in America.

What watch company marketed the Curvex?
Gruen. The company introduced the elongated, curved watch, designed to fit the wrist, in 1935.

(Gruen imported its movements from Switzerland but made its cases and assembled its watches in Cincinnati.) The watch was different from other curved watches of the time in that the movement, which Gruen called the "Curvametric," was shaped to fit the case. This meant it could be larger, and thus more accurate, than a flat movement, which would have had to fit into a small space in the middle of the case.

What was the so-called "day of two noons"?
Nov. 18, 1883, the day the United States, at the urging of the railroads, adopted Standard Time, which provided for four time zones in the United States and a fifth for the easternmost part of Canada. Before that, there were scores of different local times throughout the Unites States, based on approximations of solar time. That meant that when it was, say, 12:00 in Chicago, it was 12:24 in Cleveland. On the day of two noons, Standard Time went into effect at noon (noon Standard Time, that is). Therefore, much of the population (those in the eastern portions of their respective time zones) experienced two noons, first their old, local noon, and then the new, Standard Time one.

What watch was advertised as "The Watch with the Worm in it"?
A watch marketed by New York Standard Watch Co. The watch had a continuous screw, or "worm" gear, which took the place of a traditional lever escapement. The watch was brought to market in 1887 but the company soon opted instead for a conventional escapement.

In 1878, Waterbury Clock Co., a precursor to Timex, introduced an extremely popular watch

called the Long Wind. Why was it so named?
Its mainspring was 9 feet long (11 feet in some
models) and required 158 half-turns of the crown to
wind fully, producing a 30-hour power reserve. The
spring was coiled around the movement in the case.
The entire movement of the Long Wind rotated
inside the case, once per hour, moving the hour hand
with it. Because of its simplicity (the movement had
just 58 parts), the watch was very inexpensive; no
model cost more than $4.

**Who is considered to be "the father of the Ameri-
can watch industry"?**
Aaron Dennison (1812–1895), co-founder, with
Edward Howard, of America's first watch company,
Waltham Watch Co., in Waltham, Massachusetts, in
1850. Dennison pioneered the use of mass-production techniques in watch manufacturing, which
became the basis for America's rise as a major watch
producer after the Civil War.

What is the "American" system of manufacturing?
The method, which evolved in several industries in
the United States during the 19th century, of using
machines to produce uniform, interchangeable parts.
By the 1870s its use in American watch manufacturing resulted in products whose quality equaled or
even surpassed that of Swiss watches.

**Which U.S. company made more watches than any
other between the Civil War and World War II?**
Elgin. The company, founded in 1864, made about
40 million watches between 1867 and 1941.

When was the Elgin factory demolished?
In 1966. After the demolition, all that remained of
what was once America's most prolific watch factory,

located in Elgin, Illinois, were the main entrance posts.

When was the last major watch manufacturing plant on U.S. soil shut down?
In 2001, when Timex closed its plant in Little Rock, Arkansas, where it had manufactured cases and parts. The work was transferred to the Philippines, where Timex assembles its watches.

An incident in Kipton, Ohio, in 1891, led to the first set of uniform standards for the production of watches used by railroad employees. What happened in Kipton?
A head-on collision between a mail train and a Lake Shore & Michigan Southern Railway passenger train that was blamed on the inaccuracy of one of the engineers' watches. The crash, which killed 11 people, resulted in U.S. railroads' adopting a uniform set of requirements for watches used by railroad employees. Called the General Railroad Timepiece Standards, they included rules for the types of components used in the watches' movements as well as for the watches' precision and legibility. They also stipulated that the watches be made in America so that spare parts would be readily available.

What U.S. company was the country's best-known maker of railroad watches?
Hamilton. The company was founded in 1892, just when uniform standards for railroad watches were going into effect, and carved out a niche for itself making watches that met those specifications. It made nearly 3 million railroad watches in the decades that followed.

What U.S. watch company was well known for

such art deco models as the Piping Rock?
Hamilton. In the 1920s, the company realized it
would need to shift its attention away from the
railroad watches for which it was so well known to
wristwatches. It turned out a series of flamboyantly
stylish models of which the Piping Rock, launched in
1928, is one of the most famous.

**Two American watch companies each indepen-
dently produced watches called "The Yankee
Watch." What companies were they?**
Robert H. Ingersoll & Bro., a precursor to today's
Timex, and Hamilton Watch Co. The Ingersoll
Yankee was a pocket watch introduced in 1896. Enor-
mously popular, it sold for just one dollar and was
billed as "The Watch That Made the Dollar Famous."
The Hamilton Yankee was a commemorative wristwatch, commissioned in 1928 by Jacob Ruppert,
owner of the New York Yankees, to honor his team's
world championship that year. (Probably the most
celebrated team in baseball history, it included Babe
Ruth and Lou Gehrig.) The watch was an engraved
version of the company's Piping Rock model.

**What U.S. watch company was purchased by a
Norwegian shipping tycoon fleeing the Nazis?**
The Waterbury Clock Co., now Timex. Thomas Olsen
bought the company in 1941, soon after fleeing his
native Norway for the United States. At the time, the
company's chief business was making fuses for the war
effort. Olsen, a shipbuilder and ardent anti-fascist,
had left Norway with his family the very day the
Nazis invaded his country. With him was countryman
Joakim Lehmkuhl, an electrical engineer, author, and
publisher of an anti-fascist, pro-capitalist newspaper.
Lehmkuhl was soon put in charge of the company's
operations and remained president until 1971.

Right after Hamilton developed its Electric watch, the first battery-powered watch ever marketed, the company considered entering the toy business. What did it plan to sell?

Tiny beating "hearts" for use in children's baby dolls. To make them, the company planned to call on the battery-related know-how it had garnered while working on the Electric watch. Hamilton abandoned the idea when one toy company pointed out that little girls would be distraught at the "death" of their dolls when the hearts' batteries ran down.

What company introduced the first American-made self-winding wristwatch?

Elgin. It launched the watch in 1950 but ceased production of it soon afterward.

During World War II, U.S. watch companies converted to making war materiel and thus lost market share to the Swiss. In 1947, what percentage of watches purchased in the United States were made by U.S. companies?

About 30%. Of 7 million watches purchased, 2 million were American-made.

How did a stopwatch trigger a strike at a Massachusetts munitions factory in 1911?

The factory workers became enraged when the stopwatch was used to time their every move in an effort to improve their productivity. The stopwatch belonged to an associate of Frederick Winslow Taylor, often called "the father of scientific management." Taylor was famous for his efforts to improve workers' efficiency by analyzing the way they performed tasks and eliminating unnecessary motions and wasted time. In August 1911, at the Watertown Arsenal in Watertown, Massachusetts, Taylor's cohort performed one such "stopwatch study," as these analyses were called, on the workers there, standing by them and timing their movements to the second. They resented the process so much that they went on strike.

What U.S. watch company was founded by a former partner of Abraham Lincoln?

The Illinois Watch Co. In 1869, John Stuart, a former law partner of Abraham Lincoln, was part of a group of businessmen that founded the company in Springfield, Illinois. Another notable Illinois Watch Co. founder was John C. Adams, a major figure in the American watch industry, who also helped found Elgin Watch Co. (in 1864), the Cornell Watch Co. (1869) and the Adams & Perry Watch Manufacturing Co. (1874).

The American watch industry owed much to two men named Eli. Who were they?

Eli Whitney and Eli Terry. Whitney, famous for inventing the cotton gin, pioneered a method of mass-manufacturing guns that would lead to the "American" system of manufacturing, based on the mass production of uniform, interchangeable parts. This system became the backbone of the U.S. watch industry. Clockmaker Eli Terry was the first person to successfully apply mass-production techniques to timepiece manufacturing.

Around 1858 the company that would later become Waltham Watch Co. marketed a watch called a "chronodrometer." What kind of watch was it?

Despite its fancy name, it was simply a stopwatch. The chronodrometer was introduced during a horseracing craze that swept the country following the celebrated feats of a racehorse named Lexington. The watch's name incorporates the Greek word for racecourse, *dromos*. The chronodrometer movement sold to the trade for about $30.

What two U.S. companies teamed up to make the Data Link watch?
Timex and Microsoft. They launched the watch, which downloads data from computers, in 1995. Microsoft founder Bill Gates appeared at the press conference announcing the introduction.

What U.S. watch company built a celestial observatory in New York's jewelry district?
Bulova. The company mentioned the observatory in its 1930 annual report, noting, "the Bulova Observatory on the roof of 580 Fifth Ave., New York City, is maintained for the correct taking of sidereal time."

The Swiss watch industry received a terrible shock at the Centennial Exhibition in Philadelphia in 1876. What was it?
Proof that the U.S. watch industry was producing better watches than the Swiss were. Swiss watch companies had largely dismissed the upstart American watch industry, but received a rude awakening when they learned at the exhibition that the mass manufacturing techniques used in the United States were producing not just more watches than Swiss companies were, at lower prices, but also better ones.

What 20th-century horologist was known as "the dean of American watchmakers"?
Henry B. Fried. The son of a watchmaker, the Brooklyn-bred Fried entered the watch business at 14 and went on to become this country's most famous watchmaking teacher and the author of many watchmaking manuals that became classics. He was a

frequent contributor to watch and jewelry trade journals and compiled one of the best horological libraries in the country. When he died, in 1996 at age 89, he left his library to the American Watchmakers-Clockmakers Institute.

What did the phrase "Ball's time" refer to?
It was a synonym for extremely accurate time, and referred to the time as displayed in the shop window of Cleveland jeweler Webster C. Ball. After the United States adopted Standard Time in 1883, Ball was the first jeweler in Cleveland to display the new time as indicated by signals from the U.S. Naval Observatory in Washington, D.C. Ball later became famous in the field of railroad watches. In 1891, following a train wreck in Kipton, Ohio, blamed on an engineer's malfunctioning watch, Ball developed a system of inspection for railroad watches that was eventually adopted by 75% of this country's railroads.

A watch once owned by an American idol brought $55,000 at a Sotheby's auction in 1996. Who was the idol?
Jacqueline Kennedy Onassis. The watch was a Piaget with jade dial, diamond and emerald bezel and gold bracelet. It was sold at her much-publicized estate auction in New York in April 1996.

The New Year's Eve tradition of watching the ball drop at midnight in New York's Times Square was inspired by an older time-related practice. What was it?
The use of a so-called "time ball," a ball suspended on a pole atop a prominent building and dropped at the same time each day to signal the time. The first time ball was used in 1829, in Portsmouth, England, and the custom soon spread elsewhere. The first U.S. time

ball was dropped in 1845 in Washington, D.C., by the Naval Observatory, which continued the practice until 1936. The Times Square tradition began in 1907, when the *New York Times*, then the sponsor of the annual celebration, decided to drop a ball to mark midnight.

THE MARVELS
OF MECHANICALS

What is a Breguet balance spring?
A balance spring whose outermost coil is raised above
the plane of the rest of the spring and curved to a
smaller radius. Also called a "Breguet overcoil," it was
invented in 1795 by the great watchmaker Abraham-
Louis Breguet to make the oscillations of the balance
more equal in duration and thus improve the watch's
precision. It is still used in many high-end watches
today.

What is a "manufacture"?
A watch company that makes from start to finish at
least one of the mechanical movements it uses in its
watches. "Manufacture" (pronounced "ma nu fac
TYUR") is the French word for "factory" or "manufacturing." It confers prestige because the vast majority of watch movements are bought from outside
suppliers rather than produced in-house. The ability
to make one's own movements is considered a sign of
rare watchmaking skill.

What is a "complication"?

A watch function other than straight timekeeping. Calendars, chronographs, alarms and repeaters are all complications. A watch incorporating such functions is known as a "complicated" watch. The words "complication" and "complicated" apply to mechanical watches only; in quartz watches, abilities beyond simple timekeeping are called "functions" and the watch itself a "multifunction" watch.

What watch is the most complicated in the world?
Patek Philippe's Calibre 89. The watch has 33 complications or special features, including a split seconds chronograph, time in a second time zone, the equation of time, sidereal time, the times of sunrise and sunset, a perpetual calendar, a date-of-Easter indicator, a star chart, a moon-phase indicator, grande and petite sonneries, a minute repeater, etc., etc., etc. The movement has 1,278 parts, including 184 wheels, 61 bridges, 126 jewels and 68 springs. It is 71.5 millimeters in diameter, 28.05 millimeters thick, and weighs more than a pound. Patek made four examples of the watch, one each in yellow gold, pink gold, white gold and platinum. The company completed the first, the yellow-gold version, in 1989 to mark Patek's 150th anniversary and it was auctioned off in April of that year for 4.95 million Swiss francs (about $3 million at the time). In April 2004, a white-gold version of the watch sold at auction for $5 million. The pink gold and platinum versions are owned by an Italian collector and a Middle Eastern royal family, respectively.

What is a "grande complication" watch?
Watch purists define it as a watch that has a perpetual calendar, a split seconds chronograph and a minute repeater. Each of these complications is rare; watches that combine all three are among the most treasured

of collectors' items. In recent years, watch companies have started to use the term much more loosely, applying it to various watches with multiple "high," or difficult-to-make, complications.

How long is the average mainspring in a men's-size wristwatch?

About 8 to 12 inches. Watches with unusually long power reserves, longer than the 36 to 40 hours of most mechanical watches, have longer mainsprings. Those used in watches with power reserves of a week or more are several feet long.

How precise are mechanical watches?

The average mechanical watch gains or loses about 10 seconds per day, adding up to an error of about 5 minutes a month. However, the precision of mechanical watches varies greatly, depending on their quality and on the skill with which they have been regulated. The best mechanical watches are much more accurate than the average, gaining or losing as little as a second or two a day.

What is a chronometer?

In modern watch-industry parlance, a watch whose movement has passed a battery of timekeeping tests administered by an official testing bureau in Switzerland named COSC (Contrôle officiel suisse des chronomètres). Both mechanical and quartz watches are submitted for testing (the requirements for quartz watches are much more stringent) but the vast majority are mechanical. Historically, the term "chronometer" was used for timepieces with detent escapements (also called "chronometer" escapements), or, more loosely, for any very accurate timepiece.

How many days of testing are required for a

movement to be certified as a chronometer?
15. During that time, the movement is tested in five positions (crown up, crown down, crown to the side, face up and face down) and three temperatures (23°, 8° and 38° C, or 73.4°, 46.4° and 100.4° F).

How accurate must a movement be in order to win certification as a chronometer?
It must meet several standards of precision to be certified. The most oft-cited one is the "mean daily rate," the amount of time the watch gains or loses on average per day during two weeks of testing. That rate must not exceed -4 or +6 seconds.

How many mechanical movements receive chronometer certification each year?
About 1 million. The figure dipped about 10% in 2004 after a steady climb of several years. It passed the 1-million-mark in 2000.

What company makes the most chronometers?
Rolex. In 2004, Rolex watches received 58%, or 628,556, of the chronometer certificates issued by COSC. Rolex has long been the world leader in obtaining chronometer certificates, which it views as an important marketing tool.

How fast does a "fast-beat" movement beat?
28,800 or 36,000 half-swings, or beats, per hour. Watchmakers distinguish these movements from those that beat at 21,600 or 18,000 beats per hour because they require a different type of lubrication for their pallet jewels and escape-wheel teeth.

What do the various chimes of a minute repeater indicate?
The first series of chimes indicates the hours; the

second set the quarter hours and the third set the minutes that have passed since the last quarter hour.

Why were repeating watches invented?
So that, in the days before electricity, people could tell time at night without having to light a candle. Repeating watches chime out the time on demand, making it unnecessary to read the time from the dial.

What is the purpose of a tourbillon?
To minimize timing errors caused by the fact that a watch's balance oscillates at slightly different rates in different positions. The tourbillon consists of a small, constantly rotating cage in which the escapement and balance are set. As the tourbillon turns, the error that occurs in one position is, theoretically, canceled out by the errors in other positions. (Many watch experts believe a tourbillon serves no practical purpose in a wristwatch, whose position changes frequently while the watch is on one's wrist, thus canceling out timing errors in the normal course of wear.)

Who invented the tourbillon?
Abraham-Louis Breguet. The Swiss-born watchmaker patented the device in 1801.

What is a karussel?
A device that performs the same function as a tourbillon, i.e., canceling out timing errors caused by the effects of gravity, but which is designed to be sturdier. (Tourbillons are notoriously fragile.) A karussel is driven by the third wheel of the gear train; a tourbillon by the fourth.

What company made the first tourbillon wristwatch?
The French company Lip, in 1930.

The seconds hand of a mechanical watch appears to run in a continuous sweep but this smoothness is an illusion. Why?

In reality, the hand is moving in tiny, quick jumps—five, six, eight or 10 of them per second, depending on the balance's oscillation rate. The hand jumps once per oscillation, so on most watches, which have an oscillation rate of either 21,600 or 28,800 per hour, it will jump six or eight times per second, respectively. On a quartz watch, by contrast, the motion of the seconds hand does not appear to be continuous because the hand advances just once per second; its jumps are readily visible.

What is an "up and down" display?

A power reserve indicator, i.e., a display on the watch dial that shows how much power, in terms of running time, remains in the watch's mainspring. When the watch is fully wound, the hand on the display is in the "up" position, and as the mainspring unwinds, the hand moves gradually through an arc toward the "down" position.

What is the smallest mechanical movement ever made?

Jaeger-LeCoultre's Caliber 101, which measures just 14 by 4.8 by 3.4 millimeters and weighs less than 1 gram. It was introduced in 1929 and incorporated into watches under the Jaeger, LeCoultre and Cartier brands. (The Jaeger-LeCoultre brand did not come into being until 1937, when the Jaeger and LeCoultre firms, which had long collaborated closely with each other, merged officially.) The movement owes its small size to its being constructed on two planes (it was modeled on a 1925 movement called the Duoplan, developed jointly by Jaeger and LeCoultre). It is still used in women's watches today by brands including Jaeger-LeCoultre and Van Cleef & Arpels.

What is the Geneva Seal?

A mark of distinction given to watch movements that meet certain requirements related to the quality of their finishing. Only movements assembled in the Swiss canton of Geneva are eligible for the Geneva Seal, also called the Poinçon de Genève (stamp of Geneva), which is awarded by a group of inspectors employed by the government. The seal itself consists of the Geneva coat of arms and is inscribed on the movement.

What watch brand boasts in its advertising: "Since 1735 there has never been a quartz _____ watch. And there never will be"?

Blancpain. The brand was resurrected in 1982, in the midst of the quartz revolution, after lying dormant for many years. It was (and is) aimed at those who yearn for the old-world craftsmanship of the mechanical watch, and makes a selling point of its no-quartz history. (That history is perhaps not as impressive as the Blancpain slogan suggests: the quartz watch was not invented until the late 1960s.)

What percentage of watches exported from Switzerland are mechanical watches?

About 12%. In 2004, Swiss companies exported a total of 25.1 million finished watches, and just over 3 million of them were mechanical.

In terms of value, what percentage of Swiss watches do mechanical models represent?

About 60%. In 2004, Swiss companies exported finished watches valued at 10.2 billion Swiss francs (about $8.5 billion), and 6.1 billion Swiss francs' worth of them (about $5.1 billion) were mechanical.

What does "isochronous" mean?

That each swing of the balance wheel takes exactly the same amount of time regardless of the swing's amplitude. The closer the balance is to being isochronous, the better the watch's timing.

Which of the watch's hands is driven by the fourth wheel of the gear train?

The seconds hand. The minutes hand is driven by the center, or second, wheel, and the hour hand by a separate train, called the dial train or motion works, which converts the rotation of the minutes pinion into hours.

What is a "column-wheel" chronograph?

A chronograph whose stop, start and return-to-zero functions are controlled by a wheel that rotates in response to the pushing of the chronograph buttons. The rim of the wheel is slotted vertically, and as it rotates, the beaks of several levers enter and exit the notches, activating or deactivating the various functions. The raised sections between the notches are called "columns" (there are as many as nine on the wheel); hence the name "column-wheel" chronograph.

How does a shock-resistance device work?

It absorbs shocks that might damage the fragile pivots of the balance staff, the most vulnerable parts of a watch movement, by means of two flat springs in which the jewels of the balance staff pivots are set. When the watch is dropped or knocked, the springs absorb the shock, working much like the shock absorbers on a car.

QUARTZ QUERIES

Which company was the first to market a quartz watch?
Seiko. On Dec. 25, 1969, Seiko launched the 35 SQ
Astron, the world's first quartz watch. It was produced
in a limited series of 100 pieces, with gold cases, and
sold for 450,000 yen, or about $1,250 at the ex-
change rate of the time. Seiko claimed it was accurate
to within 5 seconds per day.

Who developed the first quartz movement?
A research laboratory called the Centre Électronique
Horloger, financed by a group of Swiss watch companies. The movement was called the Beta 21. The first
prototypes, which were completed in 1967, proved
the superior accuracy of quartz when that year they
were the top performers 10 different times at the
annual chronometry contests in Neuchâtel, Switzerland. Despite its early success with quartz technology,
the Swiss watch industry decided, after producing a
few prototypes of the new movement, not to mass-
produce finished quartz watches. It thereby ceded
victory to the Japanese industry in the early years of
the quartz revolution.

How accurate are quartz watches?
The average quartz watch is accurate to within about 10 seconds per month. However, some, including those equipped with special thermal compensation systems (the oscillation frequency of quartz crystals is affected by heat and cold) are much more precise than that, off by no more than 5 to 15 seconds per year.

Why are quartz movements so accurate?
Because the quartz resonator, a tiny piece of synthetic quartz cut in a tuning-fork shape, vibrates very fast and very steadily, much faster and more steadily than the balance wheel in a mechanical movement.

How fast does the quartz crystal in a watch vibrate?
In the vast majority of quartz watches, the crystal vibrates 32,768 times per second. In the years since quartz technology first appeared, companies have brought out a handful of quartz watches with crystals that vibrate much faster than that. (A crystal's oscillation rate depends on the crystal's size and the way it is cut.) The quartz crystal in the Omega Marine Chronometer, launched in 1974, had a frequency of 2.4 MHz (megahertz, or million times per second). The crystal in the Citizen Mega Quartz of 1975 vibrated at 4 MHz.

What is a quartz trimmer?
A device that was once used to regulate and stabilize the oscillations of the quartz crystal. Before technological advances rendered it obsolete, it was a standard feature of higher-quality quartz watches.

What two companies are the world's biggest producers of quartz watch movements?
Citizen and Seiko. For many years, the two companies have vied with each other for the title of top

quartz-movement producer, with one company winning one year and the other jumping ahead a year or two later. Recently, each company has been making more than 300 million movements a year.

What was the "Thin-Watch War"?
A competition among quartz-watch manufacturers in the late 1970s to make the thinnest watch in the world. Japan's Citizen started the war in 1978 by introducing a quartz watch 4.1 millimeters thick (the Exceed Gold). The same year, Seiko answered with a watch just 2.5 millimeters thick. Then, in 1979, the Swiss movement maker ETA outdid both with the thinnest movement yet, the Delirium, which the brands Longines, Eterna and Concord all incorporated in watches a mere 1.98 millimeters thick. (Only Concord sold the watch in the United States, under the same name as the movement.) But the war was not over; it continued until 1980, when Concord came out with the Delirium IV, just 0.98 millimeters thick. The watch was so thin it could not be worn: the case bent when the watch was strapped to the wrist.

How were the engineers at the movement maker ETA able to make the Delirium movement, launched in 1979, the thinnest movement of its time?
By eliminating the movement's bottom plate and instead attaching the parts of the movement directly to the case back.

The basic structure of the Delirium movement, the extremely thin movement introduced by ETA in 1979, was the model for another well-known quartz watch. What was it?
The Swatch. It, like the Delirium, had its movement

components attached directly to the case rather than mounted on a bottom plate. With the Delirium, the reason for the no-bottom-plate structure was to make a very thin watch; with the Swatch, the reason was to keep manufacturing costs low.

These days quartz watches can be produced at lightning speed, but it wasn't always so. How long did it take Seiko to make its first quartz watches?
Three days or more each. Manufacturing was so slow in part because the quartz crystals had to be cut and polished by hand, then, with the help of a micro-scope, ground to a precise shape and size to ensure they would vibrate at the correct frequency (8,192 cycles per second, one-quarter the speed of today's quartz crystals). Quartz-watch production speeded up tremendously when, in the 1970s, companies began to use a photochemical method for making crystals.

What company introduced the first digital watch?
Hamilton. The watch was called the Pulsar. Hamilton announced its launch with much fanfare in 1970, but technical problems kept it off the market until 1972 (the watch's display consumed so much power that the watch worked for just a very short time before it needed a new battery). When it finally became available to the public, it was a huge success despite its $2,100 price tag.

After the 1972 introduction of the world's first digital watch, priced at $2,100, prices for digital watches began to decline quickly. How long did it take them to reach $10?
Five years. In 1977, Texas Instruments introduced the cheapest digital watch yet, an LED priced at $10. Since then, prices have dipped lower still.

The first digital watches used a different type of display than those of today. What type was it?

A "light-emitting diode" (LED) display, which lit up at the touch of a button and then blinked off. By contrast, nearly all of today's digital watches have a liquid crystal display (LCD) that shows the time constantly by means of a layer of liquid crystal, sandwiched between two layers of glass or plastic.

What role does the integrated circuit play in a quartz watch?

It counts the oscillations of the quartz crystal, emitting a pulse after every 32,768 of them, i.e., once per second. In addition, it causes the crystal to vibrate by subjecting it to electric current. Depending on the watch, the IC can perform many other functions. In a digital watch, it translates the seconds it counts into the time of day and emits electronic signals to activate the time display. It also controls any extra functions the watch might have: calendar, chronograph, countdown timer, second time zone indicator, etc.

What slogan did Seiko use to advertise its quartz watches starting in the 1970s?

"Someday all watches will be made this way." The slogan turned out to be true, or nearly so: during the 1980s, quartz replaced mechanical technology almost entirely. The tagline was the backbone of an extended TV advertising blitz (the company spent $9 million on U.S. advertising in 1979 alone) that helped make Seiko a household name by the end of the 1970s.

What is an "atomic" watch?

A quartz watch that adjusts itself each night to conform to the time as measured by an atomic clock. The watch is equipped with a receiver that picks up a radio signal communicating the time as indicated by the clock (in this country, the signal is broadcast from Fort Collins, Colorado, by the National Institute of Standards and Technology). The term "atomic watch" is a misnomer, since the watch itself does not contain an atomic timekeeper. This type of watch is also called, more correctly, a "radio-controlled" watch.

The trademarked names Autoquartz and Kinetic and the generic term "motion-powered" all refer to a specific type of quartz watch. What type is it?
A watch whose electrical power is generated by a rotor that swings in response to the motions of the wearer's arm. Unlike a standard quartz watch, a motion-powered one does not have a replaceable battery. Its energy supply is replenished whenever the watch is worn, and the electricity is stored in a power cell.

In what year were the first motion-powered quartz watches introduced?
1988. That year the Japanese company Seiko launched a motion-powered watch under the name AGS (automatic generating system) and the Swiss firm Jean d'Eve incorporated its motion-powered movement into an avant-garde model called Samara.

In what year did worldwide quartz-watch production exceed mechanical-watch production for the first time?
1981. That year, 164 million mechanical watches were manufactured, versus 172 million quartz ones (114 million of these were digital and 58 million analog).

Quartz is able to perform its role as oscillator in electronic watches because it exhibits what is called the "piezoelectric effect." What does that mean?
That it both generates electricity when subjected to

stress and vibrates when subjected to an electric field. Because quartz has this quality, quartz watch crystals vibrate in response to the constant current supplied by the battery via the integrated circuit, and send back to the IC oscillating voltage, at the rate of 32,768 oscillations per second, for the IC to count into seconds.

When was quartz first used in a timepiece?
1927. That year Warren Marrison, an engineer at Bell Telephone Laboratories, developed a clock that used as its resonator a piece of quartz crystal, the first such timepiece in the world.

What percentage of chronometer certificates issued by the Swiss organization COSC are issued to quartz movements?
About 3%. In 2004, COSC gave out 1,090,581 chronometer certificates, 33,025 of which went to quartz movements.

TECHNOLOGY TIDBITS

What is the equation of time?
The difference between mean time (the time indicated on watches and clocks) and solar time (as determined by the position of the sun in the sky). This amount varies throughout the year and reaches a maximum of about 16 minutes in early November.

In our era the equation-of-time function is chiefly a curiosity or conversation piece, but it used to serve a practical purpose. What was it?
It enabled a person to set his watch by a sundial. The wearer would consult the sundial to determine solar time, and then use the equation-of-time function, which gives the difference between solar time and mean time (i.e., the time shown on timepieces) to set his watch or clock. This method worked even if the timepiece had stopped for a day or two because the equation of time would have changed little during that period.

Why will nearly all perpetual calendars made in our lifetime need to have their calendars reset in 2100?

Because the year 2100, despite being divisible by four, will not be a leap year, and perpetual calendars are designed to add an additional day to February in every year divisible by four, without exception. According to the Gregorian calendar, years that begin centuries (so-called "secular" years) and are not divisible by 400 are not leap years. A tiny number of watches have calendars designed to count just 28 days in February 2100, and hence will need no adjustment then. These are called "secular" calendars.

What is a ligne?
A unit of measurement used to denote the diameter of a watch movement. A ligne is equal to 2.256 millimeters. Its symbol is three apostrophes in a row ('").

What are watch jewels made of?
Synthetic sapphire, an extremely durable material that is also used to make scratch-resistant watch crystals. Despite their name, watch jewels, which reduce friction in the watch's movement, have almost no intrinsic value. Synthetic sapphire is mass-produced at little cost.

What is an ébauche?
An incomplete watch movement consisting of the plates, bridges and wheel train but minus the mainspring, balance and escapement. An ébauche (French for "rough draft" or "outline") is also called a "movement blank."

What do the initials "PVD" stand for?
"Physical vapor deposition," a method of applying a protective and/or decorative coating to a watch case or bracelet. The coating material, usually titanium nitride, is vaporized and deposited on the metal

substrate, to which it bonds. The resulting surface is very durable.

What makes luminous watch hands and dial markers glow in the dark?

In most newer watches, it is a substance called Super-LumiNova, which glows brightly after "soaking up" light from the sun or a light bulb (i.e., it is photoluminescent). Super-LumiNova will continue to glow for several hours or even all night if its concentration is high enough. Other watches have hands and markers coated with tritium, which does not require exposure to a light source in order to glow: it does so on its own. A layer of tritium can retain its ability to glow for decades. In some watches, tritium gas is enclosed in tiny glass vials, which are coated on the inside with phosphor and affixed to the watch dial and hands. The energy given off by the tritium makes the phosphor light up. Lastly, some vintage watches have hands and markers painted with radium, which is no longer used for this purpose because of the dangers it poses.

What is a chablon?

A kit of unassembled watch-movement parts.

What is a chaton?

A metal ring meant to hold a watch jewel.

How big is the smallest tourbillon movement ever made?

8.5 lignes (19.2 millimeters) in diameter. It was made in 1945 by Fritz-André Charrue of Le Locle, Switzerland, a one-time apprentice of tourbillon-making expert James Pellaton. Charrue spent about five years working on the movement.

Nowadays moon-phase indicators are used chiefly

as decoration, but they used to have a practical purpose. What was it?

In the days before electricity, nighttime travelers who depended on the light of the moon used them to determine when full moon would occur. Many travel clocks, especially, were fitted with moon-phase indicators.

The names "Rolls" and "Wig Wag" refer to obsolete versions of what type of watch movement?

The self-winding, or automatic, movement. The movements of these watches, introduced in 1930 and 1931 respectively, wound themselves by sliding back and forth within a frame. Blancpain made the former, under license from Leon Hatot, and Louis Müller the latter. The far superior rotor-winding system, still used in automatic watches today, soon supplanted all other types of self-winding systems.

What are blued screws?

Steel screws, used in watch movements, that have been tempered by heating them to a temperature of about 290° C, a process that turns them a deep blue color. Blued screws are popular because they are thought to be a sign of expert workmanship and are also decorative. To keep costs down, an easier chemical process is sometimes used to create them.

What was the Polyplan?

A wristwatch movement designed to fit into a curved case, introduced by Movado in 1912. The name came from the fact that it was built on multiple planes so that it conformed to the curvature of the case. The Polyplan was the forerunner of other curved-case models launched in the following decades.

MOVEMENT IMPROVEMENTS

Who developed the first reliable watch cheap enough for the working class?

Georges-Frédéric Roskopf (1813-1889) of Switzerland. In 1867, he introduced what he called a "proletarian" watch with a simplified movement that included a pin-pallet escapement rather than the jewel-pallet variety found in more expensive watches. Thanks to its economical design, it could be sold for just 20 Swiss francs (equivalent to roughly $100 today). The watch was a resounding success and was widely imitated. It and all watches like it came to be known as "Roskopf watches."

The man responsible for one important horological innovation was a close friend of Isaac Newton, with whom he performed many experiments in alchemy. What was the invention and who the inventor?

The invention was watch jewels and the inventor Nicolas Fatio (also spelled Facio) de Duillier, a Swiss mathematician and optician. In 1704 he, along with the French watchmakers Pierre and Jacob Debaufre, applied for a patent for their method of making pierced-jewel end stones for use as friction-reducing bearings at the ends of wheel staffs. Fatio met Newton in 1687, and the breakup of their friendship is said by some historians to have been the cause of a mental breakdown Newton suffered in 1692. In their years together, they devoted much time to alchemy, which fascinated both men.

For what invention is the French watchmaker Jean-Antoine Lépine best known?
A new type of caliber, invented around 1770, that was thinner than others then in existence. The thinness was due to several factors, including its having a single plate rather than the standard two. This construction came into widespread use around 1776 and is common to almost all mechanical watches made today.

One watch made in 1770 was probably the most accurate watch of its time. What made it so precise?
It had a lever escapement, the first watch in history so equipped. It was made by the English watchmaker Thomas Mudge for George III, who bought it as a gift for his wife, Queen Charlotte. Mudge claimed the watch was off by just a second or so a day. The lever escapement was as difficult to make as it was precise, and Mudge used it in just one or two other watches. It did not come into widespread use until decades after its first appearance. Today it is nearly universal.

The lever escapement represented a breakthrough when it was invented in the 18ᵗʰ century. Why?
It was the first so-called "free" escapement, meaning it eliminated direct contact between the escape wheel and the balance staff. In earlier types of escapement,

such contact interfered with the balance's oscillations.

When did the minutes hand first appear on watches?

At the end of the 17th century. The invention of the balance spring in 1675 made watches precise enough to enable the display of minutes.

When did the seconds hand first appear on watches?

In the 1690s. It did not become common until the first half of the 19th century, when better types of escapement brought major timekeeping improvements.

For what invention is the modern-day British watchmaker George Daniels known?

The co-axial escapement. The escapement was intended to lessen friction between the pallet jewels and escape-wheel teeth and eliminate the need for lubrication. Omega bought rights to use the escapement, which it has incorporated into many of its watches.

What Nobel Prize winner made two discoveries that greatly improved watches' precision?

Charles Édouard Guillaume. He won the Nobel Prize in physics in 1920 for his work with alloys, including his development of invar and élinvar, which are far less affected by temperature changes than steel. Guillaume's goal in inventing the first, invar, in the late 19th century, was to make a measurement for the meter that would not be affected by temperature (he was director of the International Bureau of Weights and Measures in Sèvres, France). Invar, a mixture of iron, nickel and manganese, found many applications, including as a material for clock pendulums and watch balances. In the 1910s, Guillaume (who had been born into a watchmaking family in the Swiss watch town of Fleurier) invented élinvar, an even better alloy (a mixture of invar, chromium and carbon), which soon became the standard material for balance springs.

What is Nivarox?
The trade name for an alloy containing iron, nickel, beryllium and other metals, first used for balance springs in the 1930s. It represented an improvement over the alloy élinvar. Today, Nivarox balance springs are made by Nivarox-FAR, a subsidiary of the Swatch Group.

What is a Glucydur balance?
A type of monometallic balance wheel, now in widespread use, made of an alloy of beryllium, copper and iron known by the trade name Glucydur. It is very hard and remains stable over a wide range of temperatures. Introduced in the 1930s, the Glucydur balance soon eclipsed the bi-metallic balance wheel.

What company developed the Gyromax balance?
Patek Philippe. The company received two patents for the balance, in 1948 and 1951. It is an adjustable-mass balance with eight weights that can be used to alter the balance's rate (a new version has just four weights). It is still used by Patek and some other high-end companies.

When was the first automatic chronograph watch introduced?
1969. That year, two self-winding chronographs were launched, one by Zenith and the other by a consortium composed of Breitling, Heuer-Léonidas, Hamilton-Buren and Dubois Dépraz. For years Zenith and

the consortium had been locked in a tight race to be the first to bring an automatic chronograph to market. Zenith won by a nose and named its watch, which was sold under the Zenith and Movado brand names (Zenith and Movado merged in September 1969), "El Primero" ("The First").

In the 17th century, two scientific geniuses both claimed credit for a very important horological invention. Who were they and what was the invention?

The inventors were the Briton Robert Hooke and the Dutchman Christiaan Huygens. The invention was the spiral balance spring (also called the hairspring), which produced a quantum leap in watches' precision, bringing their average error to within perhaps 5 minutes a day, versus 40 or 50 minutes per day previously. It was Hooke who conceived the idea, but Huygens who refined it and in 1675 incorporated it into a watch, and it is he whom most historians credit for the invention. Hooke haughtily dismissed Huygens's accomplishment, writing in his diary in 1675, "[Huygens's] spring not worth a farthing."

For what invention is Abram-Louis Perrelet best known?

A self-winding mechanism incorporating a weight that swung to and fro in response to the motion of the watch itself. This concept, which Perrelet, a prominent watchmaker from Le Locle, Switzerland, introduced in the 1770s, did not meet with much success at the time. A major reason was that pocket or pendant watches, the only types of watch then made, are usually not subjected to enough motion to make the winding weight oscillate with sufficient frequency to keep the watch's mainspring wound. In the 20th century, Perrelet's idea was resuscitated and applied to wristwatches, and it is now used universally.

What watch component declared its independence in 1776?
The seconds hand. That year, the 23-year-old Genevan watchmaker Jean-Moyse Pouzait invented the independent seconds train, making it possible, for the first time, to stop a watch's seconds hand without stopping the entire movement. Pouzait's independent-seconds-hand watch was in effect the first chronograph, although it did not have the return-to-zero function found on today's chronographs. (That invention, the work of the Nicole & Capt watch firm, would not come until 1862.)

What company owes its existence to an improved method of stem winding?
Patek Philippe. In 1842, the Frenchman Adrien Philippe introduced a new form of stem winding. Its purpose, like that of earlier stem-wind systems, was to do away with the inconvenience of winding with a key. Philippe's invention found no takers among French watch companies, so he became partners with Antoine Norbert de Patek, a Pole living in Geneva. Patek, Philippe et Cie scored a huge success with its stem-winding watches and went on to become Switzerland's most prestigious watch company.

ODDS AND ENDS

What famous psychiatrist was part owner of IWC Schaffhausen?
Carl Jung. In 1903, Jung married Emma Marie Rauschenbach, the older daughter of IWC's owner, Johannes Rauschenbach (and the second richest heiress in Switzerland). Her father died in 1905, leaving the company to his wife, his two daughters and their husbands. Profits from the company helped support Jung in the early, lean years of his career when he was receiving just a modest income as a teacher of psychiatry.

What was Sigmund Freud's connection to IWC Schaffhausen?
Freud's first patient, Fanny Moser, was married to Heinrich Moser, who was instrumental in establishing IWC in the town of Schaffhausen, Switzerland. In 1868, Moser, a watchmaker and industrialist, rented factory space to IWC founder Florentine Ariosto Jones in a facility powered by a hydroelectric power plant that Moser had built in Schaffhausen two years earlier. It was a welcome development for Jones: he had tried to set up his factory, which was to depend

on mass production, in the traditional Swiss watch-making region along the French border but failed because people feared his machine-based manufacturing methods would eliminate jobs. Freud wrote about his experience with Fanny Moser, to whom he gave the pseudonym "Emmy von N," in his 1895 work *Studies on Hysteria*.

In 1872, Japan passed a law that helped set the stage for the establishment of the country's watch industry. What law was it?

The Calendar Act, whose provisions included the adoption of Western-style timekeeping. Until then, Japanese hours varied in length according to the season, and Japanese timepieces were far different from their Western counterparts. As a result of the change, the Japanese began buying Western-style timepieces, and, in short order, making them for export.

Who was Georges-Albert Berner?

The author of the world's best-known dictionary of horological terms. Officially, his book is entitled the *Illustrated Professional Dictionary of Horology*, but it is usually referred to simply as the "Berner Dictionary." The first edition came out in 1961, followed by second and third editions in 1988 and 1994. In 1995, 19 years after Berner's death, a supplement to the dictionary, covering quartz-technology terms, was published.

What well-known watch-world figure covered the 1906 eruption of Mount Vesuvius for a Swiss newspaper?

Georges-Albert Berner, author of the famous *Illustrated Professional Dictionary of Horology*, better known as "The Berner Dictionary," published in

1961. While on vacation in his early 20s, Berner went to Naples and Pompeii to write about the eruption for a newspaper in La Chaux-de-Fonds, Switzerland, where he had studied horology.

What company is the world's oldest continuously operating watch company?
Vacheron Constantin. The company traces its beginnings to 1755, the year that master watchmaker Jean-Marc Vacheron took on his first apprentice. François Constantin joined the company in 1819, becoming the partner of Vacheron's grandson, Jacques Barthélémy Vacheron.

A Timex Indiglo watch played a hero's role in the 1993 truck bombing of the World Trade Center in New York. What was it?
The watch, which has a very bright, light-up dial, was used by investment advisor Curt Blik to lead a group of people down 38 stories through a dark stairwell.

What two watchmakers are buried in the same grave in Westminster Abbey in London?
Thomas Tompion and George Graham. The latter was the former's apprentice and close friend. Their slab is inscribed: "Here lies the body of Thomas Tompion who died November 20th, 1713, aged 75. Also Geo. Graham, Watchmaker, and F.R.S. whose curious inventions do honour to the British genius, whose accurate performances are the standard of Mechanic skill. He died the 16th of November, 1751, in the 78th year of his age."

The great watchmaker Abraham-Louis Breguet invented an early version of what music-related device?
The metronome. Breguet invented a type of metro-

nome in the late 1700s that he later improved upon with the help of composer Giovanni Paisiello, a favorite of Napoleon Bonaparte. But the invention was not a commercial success, and it was another type of metronome, incorporating a pendulum and invented in 1814 by the Dutchman Dietrik Winkel, that prevailed and is still in use today. (It's known as "Maelzel's metronome," after the German Johann Maelzel, who appropriated Winkel's invention and patented it in 1816.)

A watch auctioned off in 2001 is believed by some experts to be the oldest extant watch in the world. When was it made?
Between 1525 and 1550. The watch was made in Germany and was part of the collection owned by British banker Michael Sandberg, former chairman of the HSBC Group.

Who is Anton Bally?
Until his retirement in 2004, Bally was head of the Swatch Group's ETA subsidiary, and hence responsible for the production of roughly 100 million movements per year, as well as the Swatch brand of watches. Seldom in the public eye, Bally, an engineer, was an eminence grise at the Swatch Group. He was responsible for some of ETA's most innovative movements, both quartz and mechanical. One of his best-known projects was overseeing the development of the quartz Delirium movement, launched in 1979. Cased, the watch was a mere 1.98 millimeters thick.

How many managing directors has Rolex had since the company's birth in 1905?
Three. Hans Wilsdorf founded the company and remained at its helm until his death in 1960. André Heiniger took over until 1992, when his son, Patrick

Heiniger, became the managing director, a post he holds today.

What watch company was once owned by a sheik?
Vacheron Constantin. Sheik Ahmed Zaki Yamani, who was Saudi Arabia's oil minister for 24 years, owned Vacheron Constantin until December 1996, when he sold it to the Vendôme Group (now the Richemont Group). Yamani bought the brand in 1987.

Against what watch executive did large numbers of Swiss watchmakers stage angry demonstrations in the early 1980s?
Ernst Thomke, then general manager of the Swiss movement maker ETA. Thomke was called upon to resuscitate ETA's parent, the conglomerate Ébauches SA (part of the ASUAG group), which was near death due to competition from Japanese companies and its own inefficiency. To do so, Thomke automated manufacturing, thus eliminating thousands of jobs and incurring the wrath of laid-off workers. (He also called for the development of an inexpensive, mass-produced watch that would keep the new assembly lines rolling: the Swatch.) Thomke's hard-headed approach worked. Later, the ASUAG group merged with the other big Swiss watch conglomerate, SSIH, to form SMH, which became the engine of the Swiss watch industry revival. (Today the company is called the Swatch Group.)

Why did Audemars Piguet choose chess great Garry Kasparov as a spokesman?
Kasparov wore an Audemars Piguet Royal Oak, and had become known for his habit of taking it off at the beginning of a chess game, and later, when he saw that his opponent's end was nigh, putting it back on.

The watch company wanted to capitalize on Kasparov's conspicuous, doom-declaring gesture, so in 1996 it signed him up to appear in Audemars Piguet advertisements.

What watch brought the highest price ever at auction?

The so-called "Graves" watch, a pocket watch that Patek Philippe made for the collector Henry Graves Jr. In December 1999 it fetched $11 million at an auction at Sotheby's in New York. Graves paid 60,000 Swiss francs for it in 1933. It was the most complicated watch of its time, incorporating some 25 special functions and features. Before the Sotheby's sale, the most expensive watch ever sold at auction had been the Patek Philippe Calibre 89, which brought $3.17 million in 1989.

The Duke of Wellington believed his arch foe Napoleon to be a small-minded boor, and once adduced as proof of the emperor's pettiness his decision concerning a certain watch. What decision was it?

His decision to cancel his plan to give his brother, Joseph Bonaparte, king of Spain, the gift of a Breguet watch enameled with the map of Spain. Napoleon ordered the watch for Joseph, whom he had in 1808 installed on the throne of Spain. But in 1813, after Wellington defeated Joseph at the battle of Vittoria and caused his abdication (he moved to New Jersey in 1815), Napoleon decided not to give him the watch after all. Wellington saw this as a cruel addition of insult to injury.

SOURCES

BOOKS

Abbott, Henry G. *The Watch Factories of America: Past and Present*. Chicago: Geo. K. Hazlitt & Co., 1888.

Alft, E.C. *Elgin: An American History*. Online book published by ElginHistory.com, 2000.

Baillie, G.H. *Watches: Their History, Decoration and Mechanism*. 1929. Reprint, London: N.A.G. Press, 1979.

Baillie, G.H., Cecil Clutton and C.A. Ilbert. *Britten's Old Clocks and Watches and Their Makers*. First edition published 1899. Seventh edition, New York: Crown Publishers, Bonanza Books, 1956.

Barracca, Jader, Giampiero Negretti and Franco Nencini. *Le Temps de Cartier*. Trans. Robert Scott, Berlitz. Jouy-en-Josas, France: Fondation Cartier pour l'art contemporain, 1989.

Berner, G.-A. *Dictionnaire Professionnel Illustré de l'Horlogerie*. 1961. Reprint, Bienne, Switzerland: Societé du Journal La Suisse Horlogère, 1988.

Breguet, Emmanuel. *Breguet: Watchmakers Since 1775*. Trans. Barbara Mellor. Paris: Alain de Gourcuff, 1997.

Brunner, Gisbert L. and Marc Sich. *Heuer and TAG Heuer: Mastering Time*. Paris: Editions Assouline, 1997.

Bruton, Eric. *Clocks & Watches*. Feltham, England: Hamlyn, 1968.

Cardinal, Catherine. *The Watch, from Its Origins to the XIXth Century*. Trans. Jacques Pages. New York: Tabard Press, 1989.

Carrera, Roland. *Swatchissimo: The Extraordinary Swatch Adventure*. Geneva: Antiquorum, 1992.

Chaille, François. *Girard-Perregaux*. Trans. Deke Dusinberre. Paris: Flammarion, 2004.

Churchill, Randolph. *Winston S. Churchill, Vol. 1*. Boston: Houghton Mifflin, 1966.

Clark, Claudia. *Radium Girls: Women and Industrial Health Reform 1910-1935*. Chapel Hill, NC: University of North Carolina, 1997.

Cuss, T.P. Camerer. *The Country Life Book of Watches*. Feltham,

England: Country Life Books, Hamlyn, 1967.

Daniels, George. *The Art of Breguet*. London: Sotheby's, 1975.

Doensen, Pieter. *Watch: History of the Modern Wristwatch*. Ghent, Belgium: Snoeck Ducaju & Zoon N.V., 1994.

Dohrn-van Rossum, Gerhard. *History of the Hour: Clocks and Modern Temporal Orders*. Trans. Thomas Dunlap. Chicago: University of Chicago, 1996.

Dowling, James M. and Jeffrey P. Hess. *The Best of Time: Rolex Wristwatches, An Unauthorized History*. Atglen, PA: Schiffer, 1996.

Engle, Joel. *Rod Serling: The Dreams and Nightmares of Life in the Twilight Zone*. Chicago: Contemporary Books, 1989.

Faber, Edward and Stewart Unger. *American Wristwatches: Five Decades of Style & Design*. Atglen, PA: Schiffer, 1996.

Fallet, Estelle. *Tissot: The Story of a Watch Company*. Bienne, Switzerland: Tissot Ltd., 2002.

Fléchon, Dominique. *Baume & Mercier*. Trans. Sandra Petch. Paris: Editions Assouline, 2002.

Forster, John. *The Life of Charles Dickens*. Vol. 2. London: Dent, 1966. Entire biography first published in 1872-74 in three volumes.

Fraser, Antonia. *Faith and Treason: The Story of the Gunpowder Plot*. New York: Doubleday, Anchor Books, 1996.

Fried, Henry B. *Wittnauer: A History of the Man & His Legacy*. Short Hills, NJ: Parillo Communications, 1994.

Gilbert, Martin. *Churchill: A Life*. New York: Henry Holt, 1991.

Goodall, John. *A Journey in Time: The Remarkable Story of Seiko*. Tokyo: Seiko Watch Corp., 2003.

Grendel, Frédéric. *Beaumarchais: The Man Who Was Figaro*. Trans. Roger Greaves. New York: Thomas Y. Crowell, 1977.

Hanson, Neil. *The Great Fire of London in that Apocalyptic Year, 1666*. New York: John Wiley & Sons, 2002.

Heide, Robert and John Gilman. *The Mickey Mouse Watch: From the Beginning of Time*. New York: Hyperion, 1997.

Howard, Donald R. *Chaucer: His Life, His Works, His World*. New York: Fawcett Columbine, 1987.

Huber, Martin and Alan Banberry. *Patek Philippe Genève: Pocket*

Watches. Geneva: Antiquorum, 1982.

——. *Patek Philippe Genève: Wristwatches.* Geneva: Antiquorum, 1988.

Inge, M. Thomas (ed.). *Truman Capote Conversations.* Jackson, MS: University Press of Mississippi, 1987.

Jagger, Cedric. *Royal Clocks: The British Monarchy & Its Timekeepers.* London: Robert Hale, 1983.

——. *The World's Great Clocks & Watches.* Feltham, England: Hamlyn, 1977.

Jaquet, Eugène, Alfred Chapuis and G. Albert Berner. *Technique and History of the Swiss Watch, from Its Beginnings to the Present Day.* Trans. D.S. Torrens and C. Jenkins. Boston: Boston Book and Art Shop, 1953.

Jespersen, James and Jane Fitz-Randolph. *From Sundials to Atomic Clocks: Understanding Time and Frequency.* Toronto: General Publishing, 1999.

Landes, David S. *Revolution in Time: Clocks and the Making of the Modern World.* Cambridge, MA: Harvard University Press, Belknap, 1983.

McDermott, Kathleen. *Timex: A Company and Its Community, 1854-1998.* Timex Corp., 1998.

Moore, Charles W. *Timing a Century: History of the Waltham Watch Co.* Cambridge, MA: Harvard University, 1945.

Negretti, Giampiero. *Legendary Watches.* Trans. Rosetta Translations. Florence: Officine Panerai, 1998.

——. *Panerai Historia: From the Depths of the Sea.* Trans. Rosetta Translations. Florence: Officine Panerai, 1999.

Olsen, Kirstin. *All Things Shakespeare: An Encyclopedia of Shakespeare's World.* Westport, CT: Greenwood Publishing Group, 2002.

O'Malley, Michael. *Keeping Watch: A History of American Time.* Washington, D.C.: Smithsonian Institution, 1990.

Perret, Geoffrey. *Ulysses S. Grant: Soldier & President.* New York: Random House, 1997.

Richon, Marco. *Omega Saga.* Bienne, Switzerland: Adrien Brandt Foundation, 1998.

Roberts, Andrew. *Napoleon & Wellington: The Battle of Waterloo and the Great Commanders Who Fought It.* New York: Simon & Schuster, 2001.

Sauers, Don. *Time for America: Hamilton Watch, 1892-1992.* Lititz, PA: Sutter House, 1992.

Schama, Simon. *Citizens: A Chronicle of the French Revolution.* New York: Random House, Vintage Books, 1989.

Shugart, Cooksey, and Richard E. Gilbert. *Complete Price Guide to Watches.* Cleveland, TN: Cooksey Shugart Publications, 1997.

Simpson, Brooks D. *Ulysses S. Grant: Triumph Over Adversity, 1822-1865.* New York: Houghton Mifflin, 2000.

Sobel, Dava. *Longitude.* London: Fourth Estate, 1998.

Stadiem, William. *Too Rich: The High Life and Tragic Death of King Farouk.* New York: Carroll & Graf, 1991.

Thomson, Adam. *Time and Timekeepers.* London, 1892.

Toillon, Eveline. *Besançon: Ville Horlogère.* Joue-les-Tours, France: Editions Alan Sutton, 2000.

Tölke, Hans-F. and Jürgen King. *IWC–International Watch Co. Schaffhausen.* Zurich: Verlag Ineichen, 1987.

Uchida, Hoshimi. *History of the Japanese Clock and Watch Industry, Vol. 3, Evolution of Seiko: 1892-1923.* Tokyo: Hattori Seiko, 2000.

Veroni, Augusto. *Hublot: The Watch of Royalty.* Rome: Argo Editions.

von Osterhausen, Fritz. *The Movado History.* Trans. Derek Pratt. Atglen, PA: Schiffer, 1996.

Warhol, Andy. *The Andy Warhol Diaries.* Edited by Pat Hackett. New York: Warner Books, 1989.

Whitney, Marvin. *Military Timepieces.* American Watchmakers Institute, 1992.

PRINT ARTICLES

Balmer, Sylvie. "Ebel ouvre grand: la Villa turque." *L'Impartial,* Oct. 17, 2003.

Boynton, Robert S. "In the Jung Archives." *The New York Times Book Review,* Jan. 11, 2004, 8.

Egremont, Max. "Strange Meeting." Review of an exhibit in London's Imperial War Museum that included the poet Edward Thomas's watch. *Financial Times,* Nov. 9-10, 2002, IV.

Federation of the Swiss Watch Industry. "Sotheby's and Nelson's Watch: A Private Sale." *FH Revue.* Sept. 29, 2005, 50.

———. "Spectacular Destruction." Article on counterfeit watches. *FH Revue,* Sept. 2, 2004, 29.

"The Great Digital Watch Shake-Out." *Business Week*, May 2, 1977, 78.

Huler, Scott. "A Brief History of Time Balls." *The New York Times,* Dec. 30, 2004, 23.

Kennedy, Randy. "Hello! Say, Is That Bulgari?" A profile of ex-jewel thief Bill Mason. *The New York Times,* April 18, 2004, Sunday Styles section, 1.

König, Gerhard. "Heinrich Moser (1805-1874): A Watchmaker from Schaffhausen." *Klassik Uhren,* April 2001.

Liebeskind, David. "Rolex." A case study of Rolex written for use in a New York University business management course. 2004.

Mahaffey, James. "Suwa Seikosha's Television Watch." *NAWCC Bulletin*, February 2001, 41.

Nelson, Alan A. "The Moon Watch: A History of the Omega Speedmaster Professional." *NAWCC Bulletin*, February 1993, 33.

Thompson, Joe. "The Watch Almanac." *Modern Jeweler,* September 1990, 8WA.

———. "The Watchmakers of Sachsenhausen." *American Time,* December 1999/January 2000, 8.

Trescott, Jacqueline. "Moon Watch Resurfaces in Court." *Washington Post*, Oct. 17, 2003, C01.

WEB ARTICLES

Associated Press (AP). "Rolex From Monroe to JFK Fetches $120,000." www.comcast.net, Oct. 18, 2005.

BBC News. "Nelson Watch Sells for £400,000." www.bbc.co.uk

———. "Police Praise 'Courageous' Ozzy." Account of Ozzy Osbourne's struggle with a burglar. www.bbc.co.uk Nov. 23, 2004.

Biography Channel. "Notorious." A brief biography of the murderer Albert Walker. www.thebiographychannel.co.uk

Cambridge University. "The History of Engineering in Caius." Short biography of Gonville & Caius College graduate Sir David L. Salomons. www.cai.cam.ac.uk/alumni/famous

Casio Computer Co. "Casio Corporate History." Chapter 1: Establishment of Casio. www.casio.com

Clark, Tony, the Associated Press and Reuters. "JFK Auction Fails to Match Frenzy of Jackie O Sale." www.cnn.com/US. March 18, 1998.

Friedberg, Michael. "Harwood, Rolls, Autorist, Wig Wag & Company: Development of the Self-Winding Wristwatch." www.timezone.com

Heliosz, Edward. "Watch This Movie: Wristwatches in Movies." www.timezone.com

Hess, Jeffrey P. "An Interview with Richard Arbib." www.hessfineart.com

Lafferty, Elaine. "The Inside Story of How O.J. Lost." www.time.com. (Appeared in the print edition of *Time* magazine Feb. 17, 1997.)

Messiaen, Jean-Michel. "Pierre-Augustin Caron de Beaumarchais: Biographie développée et chronologique." www.membres.lycos.fr

Nicolet, J.C. "Questions in Time." Questions and answers on watch technology, including temperature compensation. www.europastar.com

Perez, Carlos. "Deconstructing the Ideal." A look at features that distinguish high-quality mechanical watch movements. www.timezone.com

Sears, Roebuck and Co. "Richard W. Sears, Co-Founder and 1st President." www.searsarchives.com

Shuster, William George. "Timex Ends 56 Years of Watchmaking in the U.S." www.jckgroup.com. June 22, 2001.

AUCTION CATALOGS

Antiquorum, April 12-13, 2003, Collector's Pocket Watches, Wristwatches, Clocks, Horological Tools & Documents. Article on the world's smallest tourbillon, 420.

——, Oct. 21, 1995. The Art of British Horology. Article on Josiah Emery, 146.

——, Nov. 28-29, 2001. The Art of American Horology. Article on Webster C. Ball, 112.

INDEX